HOUGHTON MIFFLIN
Math
Steps

HOUGHTON MIFFLIN

Boston • Atlanta • Dallas • Denver • Geneva, Illinois • Palo Alto • Princeton

Grateful acknowledgment is given for the contributions of

Student Book

Rosemary Theresa Barry
Karen R. Boyle
Barbara Brozman
Gary S. Bush
John E. Cassidy
Dorothy Kirk

Sharon Ann Kovalcik
Bernice Kubek
Donna Marie Kvasnok
Ann Cherney Markunas
Joanne Marie Mascha
Kathleen Mary Ogrin

Judith Ostrowski
Jeanette Mishic Polomsky
Patricia Stenger
Annabelle L. Higgins Svete

Teacher Book
Contributing Writers

Dr. Judy Curran Buck
Assistant Professor of Mathematics
Plymouth State College
Plymouth, New Hampshire

Dr. Richard Evans
Professor of Mathematics
Plymouth State College
Plymouth, New Hampshire

Dr. Mary K. Porter
Professor of Mathematics
St. Mary's College
Notre Dame, Indiana

Dr. Anne M. Raymond
Assistant Professor of Mathematics
Keene State College
Keene, New Hampshire

Stuart P. Robertson, Jr.
Education Consultant
Pelham, New Hampshire

Dr. David Rock
Associate Professor,
 Mathematics Education
University of Mississippi
Oxford, Mississippi

Michelle Lynn Rock
Elementary Teacher
Oxford School District
Oxford, Mississippi

Dr. Jean M. Shaw
Professor of Elementary Education
University of Mississippi
Oxford, Mississippi

Printed in the U.S.A.

ISBN: 0-395-98533-1

7 8 9 10 11 12 13 14 15 -PO- 07 06 05 04

Contents

UNIT 1 • TABLE OF CONTENTS

Addition and Subtraction Facts through 14

Dear Family,

During the next few weeks our math class will be learning and practicing addition and subtraction facts through 14.

You can expect to see homework that provides practice with addition and subtraction facts.

As we learn about related facts and fact families you may wish to keep the following sample as a guide.

We will be using this vocabulary:

addend one of the numbers added in an addition problem

sum result of an addition problem

difference result of a subtraction problem

fact family related addition and subtraction facts

order property Changing the order of the addends does not change the sum.
$3 + 2 = 5; 2 + 3 = 5$

grouping property Changing the grouping of the addends does not change the sum.
$3 + (1 + 2) = 6; (3 + 1) + 2 = 6$

Related Facts

$$9 + 5 = 14 \qquad 14 - 5 = 9$$

Fact Family

$$\begin{array}{r} 4 \\ + 2 \\ \hline 6 \end{array} \qquad \begin{array}{r} 2 \\ + 4 \\ \hline 6 \end{array} \qquad \begin{array}{r} 6 \\ - 2 \\ \hline 4 \end{array} \qquad \begin{array}{r} 6 \\ - 4 \\ \hline 2 \end{array}$$

Knowing addition facts can help children learn the related subtraction facts.

Sincerely,

You can write two related addition and two related subtraction facts. This is called a **fact family**.

addition facts

5 + 3 = 8
3 + 5 = 8

subtraction facts

8 – 3 = 5
8 – 5 = 3

Complete the fact family.

1.

4 + 3 = | 7 |

3 + 4 = | 7 |

7 – 3 = | 4 |

7 – 4 = | 3 |

2.
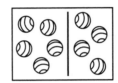

5 + 4 = | |

4 + 5 = | |

9 – 4 = | |

9 – 5 = | |

3.
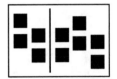

4 + 6 = | |

6 + 4 = | |

10 – 6 = | |

10 – 4 = | |

4.
3 + 5 = | |

____ + ____ = | |

____ – ____ = | |

____ – ____ = | |

5.
1 + 6 = | |

____ + ____ = | |

____ – ____ = | |

____ – ____ = | |

6.
7 + 2 = | |

____ + ____ = | |

____ – ____ = | |

____ – ____ = | |

You can write a fact family another way.
Complete.

7. $\begin{array}{r} 4 \\ + 6 \\ \hline 10 \end{array}$ $\begin{array}{r} 6 \\ + 4 \\ \hline 10 \end{array}$ $\begin{array}{r} 10 \\ - 6 \\ \hline 4 \end{array}$ $\begin{array}{r} 10 \\ - 4 \\ \hline 6 \end{array}$ 8. $\begin{array}{r} 4 \\ + 2 \\ \hline 6 \end{array}$ $\begin{array}{r} 2 \\ + 4 \\ \hline 6 \end{array}$ $\begin{array}{r} 6 \\ - 2 \\ \hline 4 \end{array}$ $\begin{array}{r} 6 \\ - 4 \\ \hline 2 \end{array}$

9. $\begin{array}{r} 3 \\ + 7 \\ \hline \end{array}$ $\begin{array}{r} \\ + \\ \hline \end{array}$ $\begin{array}{r} \\ - \\ \hline \end{array}$ $\begin{array}{r} \\ - \\ \hline \end{array}$ 10. $\begin{array}{r} 8 \\ + 1 \\ \hline \end{array}$ $\begin{array}{r} \\ + \\ \hline \end{array}$ $\begin{array}{r} \\ - \\ \hline \end{array}$ $\begin{array}{r} \\ - \\ \hline \end{array}$

**Problem Solving
Reasoning**

11. How are all the number sentences in a fact family alike?

_____

_____

✔ Quick Check

Solve.

1. $5 + 3 = 3 + \boxed{}$ 2. $4 + 6 = 6 + \boxed{}$

Complete. Then write the related addition or subtraction fact.

3. $6 - 2 = \boxed{}$ 4. $3 + 7 = \boxed{}$

_____   _____

Complete the fact family.

5. $\begin{array}{r} 7 \\ + 2 \\ \hline \end{array}$ $\begin{array}{r} \\ + \\ \hline \end{array}$ $\begin{array}{r} \\ - \\ \hline \end{array}$ $\begin{array}{r} \\ - \\ \hline \end{array}$

Name _____   **Missing Addends**

Complete.

1.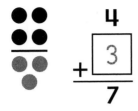
$$\begin{array}{r} 4 \\ +\ 3 \\ \hline 7 \end{array}$$

   $$\begin{array}{r} 8 \\ +\ \square \\ \hline 10 \end{array}$$

   $$\begin{array}{r} 4 \\ +\ \square \\ \hline 8 \end{array}$$

2. $$\begin{array}{r} 3 \\ +\ \square \\ \hline 5 \end{array}$$
   $$\begin{array}{r} 5 \\ +\ \square \\ \hline 9 \end{array}$$
   $$\begin{array}{r} 3 \\ +\ \square \\ \hline 8 \end{array}$$
   $$\begin{array}{r} 4 \\ +\ \square \\ \hline 10 \end{array}$$
   $$\begin{array}{r} 0 \\ +\ \square \\ \hline 0 \end{array}$$
   $$\begin{array}{r} 4 \\ +\ \square \\ \hline 7 \end{array}$$

3. $$\begin{array}{r} 3 \\ +\ \square \\ \hline 7 \end{array}$$
   $$\begin{array}{r} 2 \\ +\ \square \\ \hline 8 \end{array}$$
   $$\begin{array}{r} 5 \\ +\ \square \\ \hline 10 \end{array}$$
   $$\begin{array}{r} 2 \\ +\ \square \\ \hline 7 \end{array}$$
   $$\begin{array}{r} 2 \\ +\ \square \\ \hline 6 \end{array}$$
   $$\begin{array}{r} 6 \\ +\ \square \\ \hline 7 \end{array}$$

Complete.

4.

   $2 + \boxed{2} = 4$ $2 + \square = 7$ $2 + \square = 8$

5. $1 + \square = 5$ $1 + \square = 4$ $4 + \square = 9$

6. $6 + \square = 9$ $1 + \square = 1$ $5 + \square = 8$

7. $1 + \square = 3$ $6 + \square = 7$ $7 + \square = 8$

8. $4 + \square = 6$ $3 + \square = 5$ $3 + \square = 7$

Unit 1 • Lesson 4   (nine) 9

Complete.

9.
$$\begin{array}{r} 4 \\ + \square \\ \hline 6 \end{array}$$
$$\begin{array}{r} 2 \\ + \square \\ \hline 5 \end{array}$$
$$\begin{array}{r} 5 \\ + \square \\ \hline 8 \end{array}$$
$$\begin{array}{r} 6 \\ + \square \\ \hline 10 \end{array}$$
$$\begin{array}{r} 6 \\ + \square \\ \hline 8 \end{array}$$
$$\begin{array}{r} 5 \\ + \square \\ \hline 7 \end{array}$$

10.
$$\begin{array}{r} 4 \\ + \square \\ \hline 6 \end{array}$$
$$\begin{array}{r} 1 \\ + \square \\ \hline 7 \end{array}$$
$$\begin{array}{r} 7 \\ + \square \\ \hline 10 \end{array}$$
$$\begin{array}{r} 5 \\ + \square \\ \hline 9 \end{array}$$
$$\begin{array}{r} 1 \\ + \square \\ \hline 8 \end{array}$$
$$\begin{array}{r} 2 \\ + \square \\ \hline 9 \end{array}$$

Practice your facts. Add or subtract.

11.
$$\begin{array}{r} 9 \\ - 2 \\ \hline \end{array}$$
$$\begin{array}{r} 6 \\ - 4 \\ \hline \end{array}$$
$$\begin{array}{r} 2 \\ + 6 \\ \hline \end{array}$$
$$\begin{array}{r} 3 \\ + 7 \\ \hline \end{array}$$
$$\begin{array}{r} 7 \\ - 2 \\ \hline \end{array}$$
$$\begin{array}{r} 3 \\ - 3 \\ \hline \end{array}$$

12.
$$\begin{array}{r} 3 \\ + 1 \\ \hline \end{array}$$
$$\begin{array}{r} 9 \\ - 3 \\ \hline \end{array}$$
$$\begin{array}{r} 10 \\ - 3 \\ \hline \end{array}$$
$$\begin{array}{r} 2 \\ + 7 \\ \hline \end{array}$$
$$\begin{array}{r} 5 \\ - 4 \\ \hline \end{array}$$
$$\begin{array}{r} 2 \\ + 4 \\ \hline \end{array}$$

Problem Solving
Reasoning

13. What related subtraction fact could you use to help you find

$7 + \square = 10$? _____

★ Test Prep

Decide on an answer. Mark the space for your answer.
If the answer is **not here**, mark the space for **NH.**

14

$7 + \square = 9$

| 4 | 3 | 2 | 1 | NH |
| ○ | ○ | ○ | ○ | ○ |

10 (ten)

Unit 1 • Lesson 4

Name_____

Problem

There are **5** balls outside the box.
There are **8** balls in all.
How many balls are in the box?

1 **Understand**

I need to find out how many balls are in the box.

2 **Decide**

I can draw a picture to solve the problem.

3 **Solve**

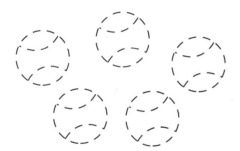
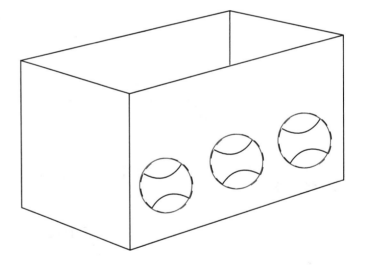

There are **3** balls in the box.

4 **Look back**

I know **5 + 3 = 8**.
My answer makes sense.

Draw a picture to solve.

1. There are **4** balls outside the box.
   There are **7** balls in all.
   How many balls are in the box?

   There are _____ balls in the box.

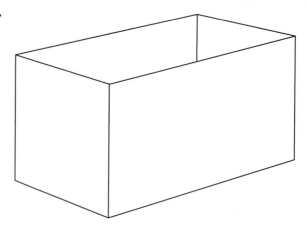

2. There are **6** balls outside the box.
   There are **10** balls in all.
   How many balls are in the box?

   There are _____ balls in the box.

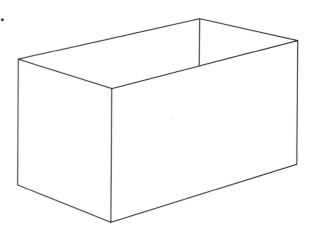

3. There are **2** balls outside the box.
   There are **8** balls in all.
   How many balls are in the box?

   There are _____ balls in the box.

   Tell why your answer makes sense.

   _____

   _____

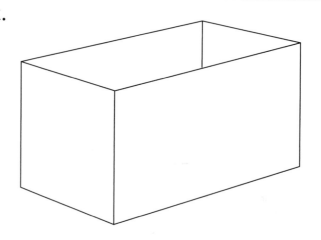

Name _____

Remember that for every fact there is a related addition or subtraction fact.

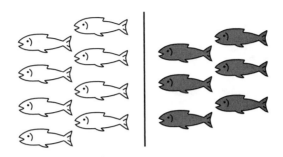

$$8 + 6 = 14$$
$$14 - 6 = 8$$

Complete. Then write a related addition or subtraction fact.

1. $5 + 8 = \boxed{13}$

    $13 - 8 = 5$

2. $14 - 7 = \boxed{7}$

    $7 + 7 = 14$

3. $8 + 4 = \boxed{}$

    _____

4. $12 - 9 = \boxed{}$

    _____

5. $13 - 7 = \boxed{}$

    _____

6. $14 - 5 = \boxed{}$

    _____

7. $5 + 7 = \boxed{}$

    _____

8. $11 - 6 = \boxed{}$

    _____

9. $6 + 8 = \boxed{}$

    _____

Complete. Then write a related addition or subtraction fact.

10.   6   14   11.   13   9
     + 8   − 8   − 4   + 4
     ‾‾14‾ ‾6‾   ‾9‾   ‾13‾

12.   5   13.   12   14.   6
     + 9   −   − 7   +   + 4   −
     ‾‾‾   ‾‾‾   ‾‾‾   ‾‾‾   ‾‾‾   ‾‾‾

Practice your facts. Add or subtract.

15. 1 + 8 = ____   18. 13 − 7 = ____   21. 5 + 7 = ____

16. 14 − 6 = ____   19. 4 + 8 = ____   22. 14 − 7 = ____

17. 9 + 3 = ____   20. 2 + 9 = ____   23. 3 + 8 = ____

Problem Solving Reasoning Solve. You can draw a picture.

24. There are **5** tops outside the box.
    There are **13** tops in all.
    How many tops are in the box?

    There are ____ tops in the box.

★ **Test Prep**

Mark next to the related fact.

   8 + 3 = 11 | ○ 11 − 3 = 8   ○ 8 − 3 = 5
               | ○ 8 − 5 = 3   ○ 11 − 4 = 7

Complete the fact family.

1.

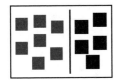

$7 + 5 = \boxed{12}$

$\underline{5} + \underline{7} = \boxed{12}$

$\underline{12} - \underline{5} = \boxed{7}$

$\underline{12} - \underline{7} = \boxed{5}$

2.

$\underline{} + \underline{} = \boxed{}$

$\underline{} + \underline{} = \boxed{}$

$\underline{} - \underline{} = \boxed{}$

$\underline{} - \underline{} = \boxed{}$

3.

$4 + 8 = \boxed{}$

$\underline{} + \underline{} = \boxed{}$

$\underline{} - \underline{} = \boxed{}$

$\underline{} - \underline{} = \boxed{}$

4.

$6 + 5 = \boxed{}$

$\underline{} + \underline{} = \boxed{}$

$\underline{} - \underline{} = \boxed{}$

$\underline{} - \underline{} = \boxed{}$

5.

$5 + 8 = \boxed{}$

$\underline{} + \underline{} = \boxed{}$

$\underline{} - \underline{} = \boxed{}$

$\underline{} - \underline{} = \boxed{}$

6.

$3 + 9 = \boxed{}$

$\underline{} + \underline{} = \boxed{}$

$\underline{} - \underline{} = \boxed{}$

$\underline{} - \underline{} = \boxed{}$

Unit 1 • Lesson 7

Write the fact family.

7.   9, 5, 14   8.   6, 8, 14

$$\begin{array}{r} 9 \\ +\,5 \\ \hline 14 \end{array} \qquad \begin{array}{r} 5 \\ +\,9 \\ \hline 14 \end{array} \qquad \begin{array}{r} 14 \\ -\,9 \\ \hline 5 \end{array} \qquad \begin{array}{r} 14 \\ -\,5 \\ \hline 9 \end{array} \qquad\qquad \begin{array}{r} 6 \\ +\,8 \\ \hline \end{array} \quad +\underline{\qquad} \quad -\underline{\qquad} \quad -\underline{\qquad}$$

Problem Solving Reasoning

9. How are all the number sentences in a fact family alike?

_____

_____

 Quick Check

Complete.

1. $3 + \boxed{} = 10$

Complete. Write a related subtraction fact.

2. $6 + 7 = \boxed{}$

_____

Write the fact family.

3.   7, 4, 11

$$+\underline{\qquad} \quad +\underline{\qquad} \quad -\underline{\qquad} \quad -\underline{\qquad}$$

You can group and add in any order.
You always get the same sum.
This is called the **grouping property**.

Add these first.

$(5 + 2) + 6 =$

$7 + 6 = 13$

Add these first.

$5 + (2 + 6) =$

$5 + 8 = 13$

Use the pictures.
Complete the number sentences.

1.

$(3 + \underline{5}) + 4 =$

$\underline{8} + 4 = \boxed{12}$

$3 + (5 + \underline{4}) =$

$3 + \underline{9} = \boxed{12}$

2.

$(4 + \underline{}) + 6 =$

$\underline{} + 6 = \square$

$4 + (4 + \underline{}) =$

$4 + \underline{} = \square$

Complete the number sentences.

3. $(3 + 6) + 3 =$

___9___ $+ 3 =$ ☐

$3 + (6 + 3) =$

_____ $+$ _____ $=$ ☐

4. $(6 + 1) + 5 =$

_____ $+ 5 =$ ☐

$6 + (1 + 5) =$

$6 +$ _____ $=$ ☐

5. $(8 + 1) + 2 =$

_____ $+$ _____ $=$ ☐

$8 + (1 + 2) =$

_____ $+$ _____ $=$ ☐

Group and then add.

6.
```
  5        2        6        4        6        5
  2        7        2        4        1        4
+ 4      + 3      + 6      + 4      + 5      + 5
```

Problem Solving
Reasoning

7. Does it matter which two numbers you add first?

Why or why not?_____

_____

★ **Test Prep**

Decide on an answer. Mark the space for your answer.
If the answer is **not here**, mark the space for **NH**.

8

$(5 + 2) + 6 =$ ☐

11	12	13	15	NH
○	○	○	○	○

18 (eighteen)

Unit 1 • Lesson 8

Name _____   **Three Addends**

Add.

1.
$$
\begin{array}{r} 2 \\ 4 \\ + 3 \\ \hline \end{array} \!\! 6 \qquad
\begin{array}{r} 1 \\ 1 \\ + 7 \\ \hline \end{array} \qquad
\begin{array}{r} 5 \\ 4 \\ + 4 \\ \hline \end{array} \qquad
\begin{array}{r} 6 \\ 2 \\ + 2 \\ \hline \end{array} \qquad
\begin{array}{r} 1 \\ 2 \\ + 5 \\ \hline \end{array} \qquad
\begin{array}{r} 2 \\ 4 \\ + 6 \\ \hline \end{array}
$$
9

2.
$$
\begin{array}{r} 3 \\ 5 \\ + 2 \\ \hline \end{array} \!\! 7 \qquad
\begin{array}{r} 4 \\ 1 \\ + 6 \\ \hline \end{array} \qquad
\begin{array}{r} 6 \\ 1 \\ + 2 \\ \hline \end{array} \qquad
\begin{array}{r} 1 \\ 4 \\ + 3 \\ \hline \end{array} \qquad
\begin{array}{r} 5 \\ 4 \\ + 5 \\ \hline \end{array} \qquad
\begin{array}{r} 7 \\ 1 \\ + 2 \\ \hline \end{array}
$$

3.
$$
\begin{array}{r} 8 \\ 4 \\ + 0 \\ \hline \end{array} \qquad
\begin{array}{r} 1 \\ 7 \\ + 2 \\ \hline \end{array} \qquad
\begin{array}{r} 2 \\ 3 \\ + 6 \\ \hline \end{array} \qquad
\begin{array}{r} 2 \\ 4 \\ + 0 \\ \hline \end{array} \qquad
\begin{array}{r} 8 \\ 1 \\ + 4 \\ \hline \end{array} \qquad
\begin{array}{r} 4 \\ 2 \\ + 2 \\ \hline \end{array}
$$

4.
$$
\begin{array}{r} 3 \\ 4 \\ + 3 \\ \hline \end{array} \qquad
\begin{array}{r} 3 \\ 6 \\ + 2 \\ \hline \end{array} \qquad
\begin{array}{r} 1 \\ 1 \\ + 8 \\ \hline \end{array} \qquad
\begin{array}{r} 0 \\ 5 \\ + 4 \\ \hline \end{array} \qquad
\begin{array}{r} 5 \\ 2 \\ + 6 \\ \hline \end{array} \qquad
\begin{array}{r} 6 \\ 3 \\ + 1 \\ \hline \end{array}
$$

5.
$$
\begin{array}{r} 5 \\ 5 \\ + 3 \\ \hline \end{array} \qquad
\begin{array}{r} 3 \\ 5 \\ + 2 \\ \hline \end{array} \qquad
\begin{array}{r} 4 \\ 6 \\ + 2 \\ \hline \end{array} \qquad
\begin{array}{r} 3 \\ 4 \\ + 0 \\ \hline \end{array} \qquad
\begin{array}{r} 6 \\ 2 \\ + 1 \\ \hline \end{array} \qquad
\begin{array}{r} 2 \\ 8 \\ + 0 \\ \hline \end{array}
$$

Complete.

6.
$$\begin{array}{r} 2 \\ 2 \\ + \boxed{5} \\ \hline 9 \end{array}$$
$$\begin{array}{r} 2 \\ 4 \\ + \boxed{} \\ \hline 11 \end{array}$$
$$\begin{array}{r} 1 \\ 3 \\ + \boxed{} \\ \hline 9 \end{array}$$
$$\begin{array}{r} 4 \\ 3 \\ + \boxed{} \\ \hline 12 \end{array}$$
$$\begin{array}{r} 6 \\ 1 \\ + \boxed{} \\ \hline 10 \end{array}$$
$$\begin{array}{r} 7 \\ 0 \\ + \boxed{} \\ \hline 12 \end{array}$$

7.
$$\begin{array}{r} 4 \\ 1 \\ + \boxed{} \\ \hline 13 \end{array}$$
$$\begin{array}{r} 1 \\ 6 \\ + \boxed{} \\ \hline 14 \end{array}$$
$$\begin{array}{r} 2 \\ 5 \\ + \boxed{} \\ \hline 10 \end{array}$$
$$\begin{array}{r} 3 \\ 2 \\ + \boxed{} \\ \hline 9 \end{array}$$
$$\begin{array}{r} 4 \\ 2 \\ + \boxed{} \\ \hline 13 \end{array}$$
$$\begin{array}{r} 0 \\ 8 \\ + \boxed{} \\ \hline 9 \end{array}$$

Practice your facts. Add or subtract.

8.
$$\begin{array}{r} 13 \\ - 7 \\ \hline \end{array}$$
$$\begin{array}{r} 8 \\ + 3 \\ \hline \end{array}$$
$$\begin{array}{r} 13 \\ - 9 \\ \hline \end{array}$$
$$\begin{array}{r} 6 \\ + 7 \\ \hline \end{array}$$
$$\begin{array}{r} 13 \\ - 6 \\ \hline \end{array}$$
$$\begin{array}{r} 13 \\ - 8 \\ \hline \end{array}$$

9.
$$\begin{array}{r} 6 \\ + 5 \\ \hline \end{array}$$
$$\begin{array}{r} 9 \\ + 4 \\ \hline \end{array}$$
$$\begin{array}{r} 11 \\ - 2 \\ \hline \end{array}$$
$$\begin{array}{r} 12 \\ - 8 \\ \hline \end{array}$$
$$\begin{array}{r} 5 \\ + 8 \\ \hline \end{array}$$
$$\begin{array}{r} 14 \\ - 7 \\ \hline \end{array}$$

★ Test Prep

Decide on an answer. Mark the space for your answer. If the answer is **not here**, mark the space for **NH**.

10
$$\begin{array}{r} 5 \\ 2 \\ + 6 \\ \hline \boxed{} \end{array}$$

11	12	13	14	NH
○	○	○	○	○

20 (twenty)

Unit 1 • Lesson 9

Name _____

Ring the facts that name the number on the house.

1.

11

(9 + 2)	(8 + 3)
8 + 4	7 + 5
5 + 8	(6 + 5)
6 + 7	3 + 7
(4 + 7)	9 + 3

2.

14

6 + 8	7 + 5
8 + 3	4 + 8
9 + 3	7 + 7
5 + 9	10 + 4
3 + 9	4 + 7

3.

13

9 + 4	7 + 6
3 + 6	4 + 9
8 + 5	5 + 8
9 + 3	7 + 5
8 + 4	6 + 7

Make the facts name the number on the umbrella.

4.

13

4 + _9_ | ___ + 6
6 + ___ | ___ + 4
5 + ___ | ___ + 7
9 + ___ | ___ + 5
3 + ___ | ___ + 8

5.

12

6 + ___ | ___ + 2
8 + ___ | ___ + 6
5 + ___ | ___ + 9
9 + ___ | ___ + 5
7 + ___ | ___ + 4

6.

11

6 + ___ | ___ + 9
4 + ___ | ___ + 8
5 + ___ | ___ + 7
3 + ___ | ___ + 4
2 + ___ | ___ + 6

Unit 1 • Lesson 10

Ring the ways to name the number.

7. 13 | 4 + 2 + 3   3 + 7 + 3   4 + 6   5 + 4 + 4

8. 14 | 6 + 3 + 5   4 + 2 + 4   1 + 8 + 5   7 + 6

Problem Solving
Reasoning

9. How many different ways can you name 10? List them.

_____

_____

_____

 Quick Check

Solve.

1. 6 + (2 + 2) = ☐

2. 3
    3
  + 2
  ─────

3. 4
    5
  + 3
  ─────

Ring the ways to name 12.

4. 8 + 4 | 6 + 5
   7 + 7 | 6 + 6
   9 + 2 | 5 + 7
   2 + 10 | 3 + 8

Name _____

2 is not equal to **5**
2 ≠ 5

3 is equal to **3**
3 = 3

Use = or ≠.

1.

2 (=) 2

14 ( ) 14

11 ( ) 7

9 ( ) 9

12 ( ) 13

2. **Think 8.**

4 + 4 (≠) 5

2 + 8 ( ) 9

7 + 5 ( ) 12

7 + 3 ( ) 14

10 − 5 ( ) 3

Use = or ≠.

3. $2 + 3$ ⬤≠ 4 4. $3 + 4$ ◯ 7 5. $6 - 4$ ◯ 3

$11 - 7$ ◯ 4 $5 + 6$ ◯ 4 $7 + 2$ ◯ 9

$14 - 7$ ◯ 5 $9 - 6$ ◯ 3 $13 - 5$ ◯ 2

Use + or −.

6.
$$\begin{array}{r} 14 \\ \ominus\,8 \\ \hline 6 \end{array} \quad \begin{array}{r} 8 \\ \bigcirc4 \\ \hline 12 \end{array} \quad \begin{array}{r} 9 \\ \bigcirc2 \\ \hline 7 \end{array} \quad \begin{array}{r} 12 \\ \bigcirc3 \\ \hline 9 \end{array} \quad \begin{array}{r} 10 \\ \bigcirc4 \\ \hline 6 \end{array} \quad \begin{array}{r} 0 \\ \bigcirc9 \\ \hline 9 \end{array}$$

7. 5 ◯ $9 = 14$ 13 ◯ $4 = 9$ 9 ◯ $4 = 5$

Use = or ≠.

8. $2 + 6$ ⬤= $14 - 6$ 9. $3 + 5$ ◯ $8 - 4$

$7 - 3$ ◯ $2 + 2$ $13 - 9$ ◯ $2 + 7$

★ Test Prep

Which of these is not true? Mark the space next to your answer.

⑩

○ $8 ≠ 3 + 3$ ○ $12 - 9 ≠ 4$

○ $13 = 4 + 9$ ○ $6 + 6 = 14$

24 (twenty-four)   Unit 1 • Lesson 11

Tim has **5** shells.

5 is greater than **3**. **5 > 3**

Sue has **3** shells.

3 is less than **5**. **3 < 5**

Use > or <.

1. 9 (>) 6   12 (<) 14   13 (>) 10

2. 6 ( ) 8   13 ( ) 7   4 ( ) 5

3. 9 ( ) 12   7 ( ) 4   7 ( ) 9

4. 6 ( ) 9   4 ( ) 9   8 ( ) 14

5. 4 ( ) 8   7 ( ) 13   9 ( ) 5

6. 3 ( ) 6   12 ( ) 5   6 ( ) 12

7. 8 ( ) 5   6 ( ) 5   5 ( ) 3

8. 6 ( ) 7   9 ( ) 4   2 ( ) 8

Tim has **5** shells.

Sue has **5** shells.

5 is equal to **5**.   **5 = 5**

Use >, <, or =.

9.
14 (>) 6   3 (=) 3   8 (<) 12

10.
11 ( ) 11   14 ( ) 5   9 ( ) 9

11.
9 ( ) 13 − 4   8 ( ) 2 + 4   5 ( ) 8 − 3

12.
12 ( ) 6 + 8   10 ( ) 4 + 6   14 ( ) 8 + 5

Problem Solving
Reasoning

13. 3 + 3 (>) 6

Is the answer correct? Why or why not?_____

_____

★ Test Prep

Which of these is not true? Mark the space for your answer.

14

11 > 9 + 2   7 = 7   5 < 8 + 4   14 = 8 + 6
○   ○   ○   ○

26 (twenty-six)

Unit 1 • Lesson 12

Write + or −. Then solve.

1. Pam has **2** red balls.
   Sue has **4** purple balls.
   José has **3** orange balls.
   How many balls do they have
   in all?

   Think Do you need to add or
   subtract to find the answer?

   ___add___

   2 (+) 4 (+) 3 = ____

   Answer ____ balls

2. Ted has **10** tops.
   7 spin away.
   How many tops are left?

   Think Do you need to add or
   subtract to find the answer?

   _____

   10 ( ) 7 = ____

   Answer ____ tops

3. There are **8** white cats.
   There are **4** black cats.
   There are **2** brown cats.
   How many cats in all?

   8 ( ) 4 ( ) 2 = ____

   Answer ____ cats

4. There are **8** birds.
   3 fly away.
   How many birds
   are left?

   8 ( ) 3 = ____

   Answer ____ birds

5. There are **8** green fish.
   There are **3** yellow fish.
   How many fish in all?

   8 ( ) 3 = ____

   Answer ____ fish

6. There are **8** green fish.
   There are **3** yellow fish.
   How many more green fish are
   there than yellow fish?

   8 ( ) 3 = ____

   Answer ____ more green fish

Solve.

7. There are **5** boys and **4** girls at the party. How many children are there in all?

5 ◯ 4 = ____

Answer ____ children

8. Mom has **10** apples. The children eat **8** of them. How many apples are left?

10 ◯ 8 = ____

Answer ____ apples

9. We have **3** red hats, **4** blue hats, and **2** green hats. How many hats are there in all?

____ ◯ ____ ◯ ____ = ____

Answer ____ hats

10. **Seven** of the children have white socks. **Two** of the children have blue. How many more children have white socks than blue socks?

____ ◯ ____ = ____

Answer ____ more children

Extend Your Thinking

11. Draw a picture to match one of the problems.

Which problem did you choose? _____
Does your picture show addition or subtraction? _____

Complete the tables.

1. Add 2.

8	10
0	2
4	6
7	9
5	7

2. Add 3.

7	
6	
5	
8	
9	

3. Add 5.

6	
4	
9	
3	
8	

4. Subtract 5.

10	5
14	
11	
13	
12	

5. Subtract 4.

11	
14	
10	
12	
8	

6. Subtract 7.

14	
11	
13	
10	
12	

Complete the rule.

7. Subtract __5__.

9	4
11	6
12	7
14	9
13	8

8. Add ____.

6	12
8	14
3	9
5	11
4	10

9. Subtract ____.

14	7
10	3
9	2
13	6
11	4

Complete the rule.

10. Subtract ____.

12	9
9	6
10	7
13	10
11	8

11. Add ____.

9	13
4	8
7	11
10	14
6	10

12. Subtract ____.

14	6
13	5
12	4
11	3
10	2

Problem Solving
Reasoning

13. How can you check to see if your rule is correct?

_____

_____

✓ Quick Check

Use = or ≠.

1. $3 + 8$ ◯ 12

Use >, <, or =.

2. $14 - 7$ ◯ $3 + 3$

Complete the table.

3.   Add 6.

6	
4	
7	

Name _____

Complete. Then write a related addition or subtraction fact.

1. $4 + 7 = \boxed{}$ 2. $14 - 6 = \boxed{}$ 3. $8 + 2 = \boxed{}$

_____   _____   _____

Complete the fact family.

4. $\begin{array}{r} 7 \\ + 2 \\ \hline \end{array}$ $+$ ___ $-$ ___ $-$ ___

5. $\begin{array}{r} 8 \\ + 6 \\ \hline \end{array}$ $+$ ___ $-$ ___ $-$ ___

6. $\begin{array}{r} 7 \\ + 6 \\ \hline \end{array}$ $+$ ___ $-$ ___ $-$ ___

7. $\begin{array}{r} 4 \\ + 3 \\ \hline \end{array}$ $+$ ___ $-$ ___ $-$ ___

Solve.

8. $\begin{array}{r} 5 \\ + 3 \\ \hline \end{array}$ 9. $\begin{array}{r} 8 \\ + 4 \\ \hline \end{array}$ 10. $\begin{array}{r} 6 \\ + 2 \\ \hline \end{array}$ 11. $\begin{array}{r} 9 \\ + 5 \\ \hline \end{array}$ 12. $\begin{array}{r} 7 \\ + 7 \\ \hline \end{array}$ 13. $\begin{array}{r} 6 \\ + 6 \\ \hline \end{array}$

14. $\begin{array}{r} 14 \\ - 5 \\ \hline \end{array}$ 15. $\begin{array}{r} 12 \\ - 7 \\ \hline \end{array}$ 16. $\begin{array}{r} 10 \\ - 8 \\ \hline \end{array}$ 17. $\begin{array}{r} 11 \\ - 7 \\ \hline \end{array}$ 18. $\begin{array}{r} 13 \\ - 6 \\ \hline \end{array}$ 19. $\begin{array}{r} 12 \\ - 8 \\ \hline \end{array}$

Solve.

20.
$$\begin{array}{r} 8 \\ + \square \\ \hline 10 \end{array}$$

21.
$$\begin{array}{r} 4 \\ + \square \\ \hline 9 \end{array}$$

22.
$$\begin{array}{r} 5 \\ + \square \\ \hline 7 \end{array}$$

23.
$$\begin{array}{r} 4 \\ + \square \\ \hline 8 \end{array}$$

Use >, <, or =.

24. 7 ◯ 13   25. 9 ◯ 9   26. 5 ◯ 12

27. 4 + 4 ◯ 12 – 4   28. 14 ◯ 6 + 5   29. 8 ◯ 9 + 2

Add.

30.
$$\begin{array}{r} 4 \\ 1 \\ + 5 \\ \hline \end{array}$$

31.
$$\begin{array}{r} 3 \\ 4 \\ + 2 \\ \hline \end{array}$$

32.
$$\begin{array}{r} 6 \\ 4 \\ + 4 \\ \hline \end{array}$$

33.
$$\begin{array}{r} 7 \\ 2 \\ + 4 \\ \hline \end{array}$$

Problem Solving Reasoning Solve.

34. Luis has **7** books. He buys **6** more books. How many books does he have in all?

____ ◯ ____ = ____

_____ books

35. Jackie has **8** toy cars. She gives **2** of them to a friend. How many cars does she have left?

____ ◯ ____ = ____

_____ cars

Unit 1 • Review

1

6 + 7 = 13

○ 6 + 8 = 14   ○ 13 − 8 = 5

○ 13 − 7 = 6   ○ 7 + 7 = 14

2

$$\begin{array}{r} 6 \\ +\ \square \\ \hline 10 \end{array}$$

8   7   6   4
○   ○   ○   ○

3

13 − 4 < 8   6 < 14   8 > 5 + 7   9 = 7
○   ○   ○   ○

4

8 tops   10 tops   12 tops   14 tops
○   ○   ○   ○

Decide on an answer. Mark the space for your answer.
If the answer is **not here**, mark **NH**.

5

$$8 + 5 = \square$$

9	10	11	12	NH
○	○	○	○	○

6

$$11 - 8 = \square$$

2	3	5	6	NH
○	○	○	○	○

7

$$\begin{array}{r} 5 \\ +\,4 \\ \hline \square \end{array}$$

7	8	9	10	NH
○	○	○	○	○

8

$$\begin{array}{r} 6 \\ +\,\square \\ \hline 14 \end{array}$$

2	4	5	8	NH
○	○	○	○	○

9

$$\begin{array}{r} 3 \\ 3 \\ +\,7 \\ \hline \square \end{array}$$

10	12	13	14	NH
○	○	○	○	○

10

$$12 \bigcirc 7 = 5$$

+	−	>	<	NH
○	○	○	○	○

34 (thirty-four)

Unit 1 • Cumulative Review

UNIT 2 • TABLE OF CONTENTS

Place Value through 100

UNIT 2 • TABLE OF CONTENTS

Dear Family,

During the next few weeks our math class will be learning about place value through 100 and money amounts through 99¢.

You can expect to see homework that provides practice with place value and money amounts.

As we learn about place value and money amounts, you may wish to keep the following sample as a guide.

Place Value

Money Amounts

In **50¢** there are **5** dimes.

In **50¢** there are **50** pennies.

Knowing place value can help children with their addition and subtraction exercises.

Sincerely,

1 group of **10** ones is **1** ten.

Complete.

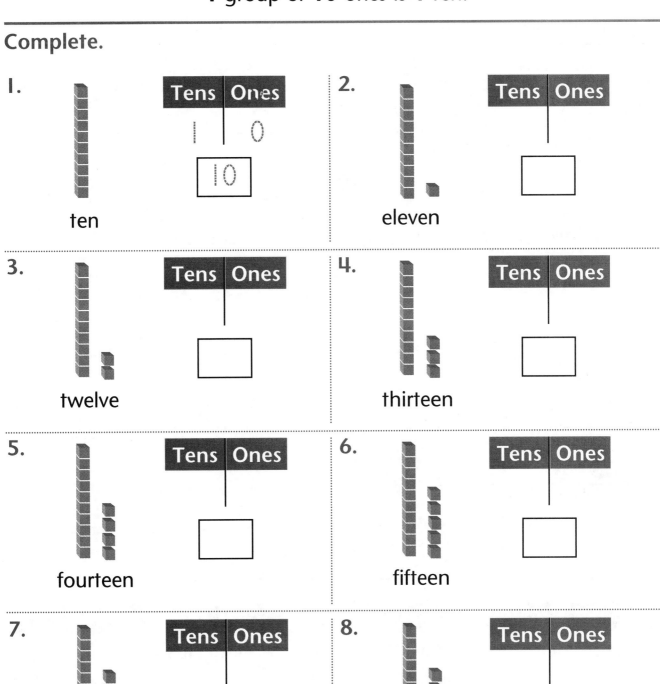

1.
Tens	Ones
1	0

10

ten

2.
Tens	Ones

eleven

3.
Tens	Ones

twelve

4.
Tens	Ones

thirteen

5.
Tens	Ones

fourteen

6.
Tens	Ones

fifteen

7.
Tens	Ones

sixteen

8.
Tens	Ones

seventeen

Unit 2 • Lesson 1

Complete.

9.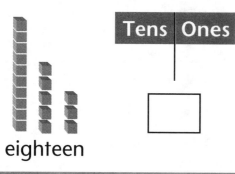

eighteen

Tens	Ones

10.

nineteen

Tens	Ones

What comes

11.

after?	before?	between?	before and after?
16, _17_	_17_, 18	16, _17_, 18	_13_, 14, _15_
13, ____	____, 15	10, ____, 12	____, 18, ____

Ring the greatest number. | Ring the least number.

12.   **19,   14, 7**

13.   **12,   11, 18**

Use >, <, or =.

14. **10** ⬤< **15** | 15. **11** ◯ **10** | 16. **12** ◯ **12** | 17. **13** ◯ **17**

Problem Solving
Reasoning

18. Which number is greater, 13 or 15? Why? _____

_____

★ Test Prep

What number is missing? Mark the space for your answer.

19

13, ____, 15 | **12**   **13**   **14**   **15**
                          ◯   ◯   ◯   ◯

38 (thirty-eight)

Unit 2 • Lesson 1

Name _____

Complete.

1.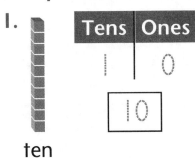

Tens	Ones
1	0

10

ten

2.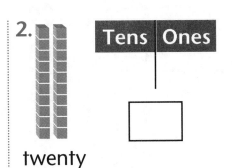

Tens	Ones

twenty

3.

Tens	Ones

thirty

4.

Tens	Ones

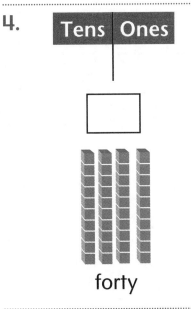

forty

5.

Tens	Ones

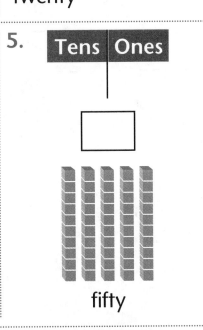

fifty

6.

Tens	Ones

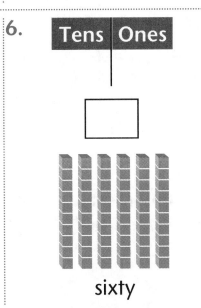

sixty

7.

Tens	Ones

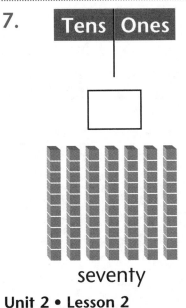

seventy

8.

Tens	Ones

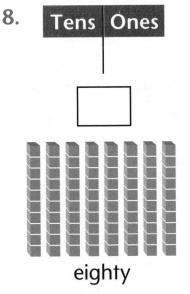

eighty

9.

Tens	Ones

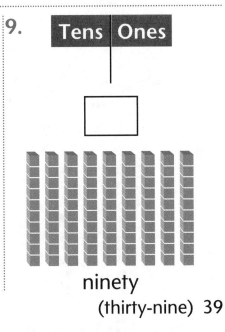

ninety

Unit 2 • Lesson 2

Complete.

10.

Tens	Ones	
6	0	60
2	0	
9	0	
4	0	
1	0	
5	0	
8	0	
3	0	
7	0	

11.

	Tens	Ones
20	2	0
50		
90		
70		
60		
10		
40		
80		
30		

Problem Solving
Reasoning

12. How many ones are in 2 tens? _____
    Draw a picture to show how you know.

★ Test Prep

What is the number? Mark the space for your answer.

13

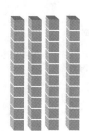

20	30	40	50
○	○	○	○

40 (forty)

Complete.

1.

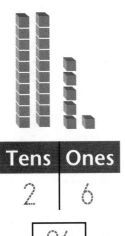

Tens	Ones
2	6

26

2.

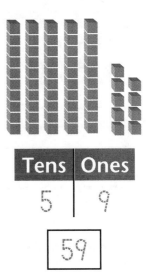

Tens	Ones
5	9

59

3.

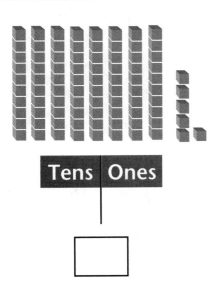

Tens	Ones

4.

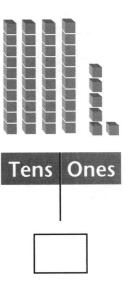

Tens	Ones

Write the numbers.

5. **4** tens and **5** ones 45

6. **8** tens and **9** ones _____

7. **2** tens and **0** ones _____

8. **4** tens and **4** ones _____

Complete.

9.

	Tens	Ones
21	2	1
55		
11		
67		

10.

Tens	Ones	
7	3	73
9	2	
2	7	
4	0	

✓ **Quick Check**

Write the number.

1.

10		30	40		60	70	80	

2.

3.

Tens	Ones	
4	3	= ___

Tens	Ones	
8	7	= ___

4. Write how many tens and ones.

48 =

Tens	Ones

96 =

Tens	Ones

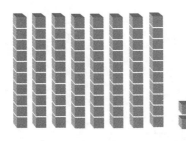

8 tens and **2** ones

80 + 2 = 82

8 tens and **2** ones is the same as **80 + 2 = 82.**

Complete.

1. **2** tens and **1** one $\boxed{20}$ + $\boxed{1}$ = $\boxed{}$

2. **9** tens and **3** ones $\boxed{}$ + $\boxed{}$ = $\boxed{}$

3. **4** tens and **9** ones $\boxed{}$ + $\boxed{}$ = $\boxed{}$

4. **6** tens and **7** ones $\boxed{}$ + $\boxed{}$ = $\boxed{}$

5. **20 + 3 =** $\boxed{2}$ tens and $\boxed{3}$ ones = $\boxed{}$

6. **80 + 8 =** $\boxed{}$ tens and $\boxed{}$ ones = $\boxed{}$

7. **0 + 4 =** $\boxed{}$ tens and $\boxed{}$ ones = $\boxed{}$

8. **70 + 5 =** $\boxed{}$ tens and $\boxed{}$ ones = $\boxed{}$

9. **23 =** $\boxed{}$ tens and $\boxed{}$ ones

10. **79 =** $\boxed{}$ tens and $\boxed{}$ ones

11. **46 =** $\boxed{}$ tens and $\boxed{}$ ones

12. **83 =** $\boxed{}$ tens and $\boxed{}$ ones

13. **33 =** $\boxed{}$ tens and $\boxed{}$ ones

14. **96 =** $\boxed{}$ tens and $\boxed{}$ ones

15. **74 =** $\boxed{}$ tens and $\boxed{}$ ones

16. **65 =** $\boxed{}$ tens and $\boxed{}$ ones

Complete.

17. $10 + 9 =$ ☐ 19

18. ☐ 10 $+ 8 = 18$

19. $20 + 7 =$ ☐

20. ☐ $+ 7 = 77$

21. $40 + 8 =$ ☐

22. ☐ $+ 3 = 43$

23. $70 + 1 =$ ☐

24. ☐ $+ 2 = 92$

Fill in the blanks.

25. **23** means ___2___ tens and ___3___ ones   or ___20___ $+$ ___3___.

26. **60** means ____ tens and ____ ones   or ____ $+$ ____.

27. **5** means ____ tens and ____ ones   or ____ $+$ ____.

Problem Solving
Reasoning

28. How are the numbers **29** and **92** alike? How are they different?

_____

_____

★ **Test Prep**

Decide on an answer. Mark the space for your answer.
If the answer is **not here**, mark the space for **NH**.

29

$40 + 3 =$ ☐

    23   36   43   53   NH
    ○   ○   ○   ○   ○

Unit 2 • Lesson 4

Name _____

Count to 100. Complete the hundred chart.
Think about what numbers come before, after, and between.

1.

1	2		4					9	
		13		15			18		
21	22	23	24	25	26	27	28	29	30
31		33	34		37				
	42			45					
	53								
61					66				
	72							79	
81					86				
	92								100

Write the missing numbers.

2. 30, _____, _____, 33, _____, 35, _____, _____, 38, _____

3. 40, _____, _____, 43, 44, _____, _____, 47, _____, _____,

Unit 2 • Lesson 5   (forty-five) 45

What comes before?

4. __80__ , 81

____ , 30

____ , 56

5. __24__ , 25

____ , 69

____ , 38

6. ____ , 40

____ , 81

____ , 26

What comes after?

7. 63, __64__

89, ____

40, ____

8. 98, __99__

85, ____

47, ____

9. 50, ____

64, ____

88, ____

What comes between?

10. 25, __26__ , 27

49, ____ , 51

30, ____ , 32

11. 23, ____ , 25

38, ____ , 40

60, ____ , 62

12. 32, ____ , 34

58, ____ , 60

97, ____ , 99

Problem Solving Reasoning Use the hundred chart.

13. What number is **10** more than **62**? ____

14. What number is **10** less than **54**? ____

15. What number is **1** more than **99**? ____

★ Test Prep

Which number is between 64 and 66?
Mark the space for your answer.

45 ○   53 ○   61 ○   65 ○

Name_____

Problem

How many stamps are there?

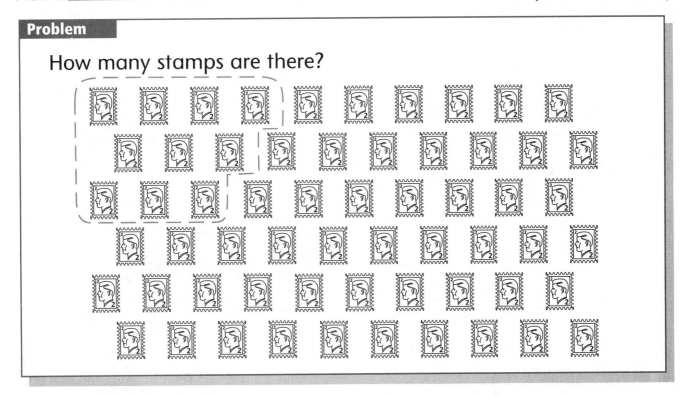

1 **Understand**

I need to find out how many stamps there are.

2 **Decide**

I can guess then check.

3 **Solve**

I'll think about **10** to help me guess.

My guess is _____ stamps.
I will ring groups of **10**.
I will count to check.

There are _____ stamps.

4 **Look back**

Does my answer make sense?

Unit 2 • Lesson 6

(forty-seven) 47

How many are there?
Guess, then check.

1.

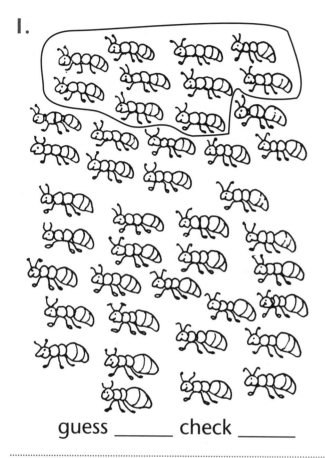

guess _____ check _____

2.

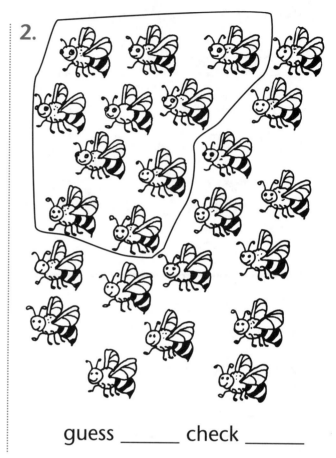

guess _____ check _____

3.

guess _____ check _____

4.

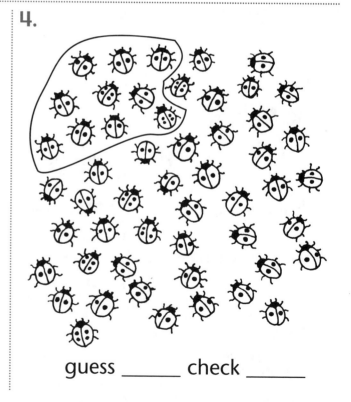

guess _____ check _____

Name_____

Count by 2's.

1.

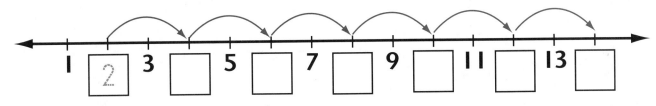

1 2 3 □ 5 □ 7 □ 9 □ 11 □ 13 □

2. 2, __4__ , 6, _____ , _____ , _____ , 14, _____ , _____ , 20,

22, _____ , 26, _____ , _____ , 32, _____ , _____ , _____ , _____ ,

_____ ,44, _____ , _____ , _____ , _____ ,54, _____ , _____ , _____ ,

Count by 3's.

3.

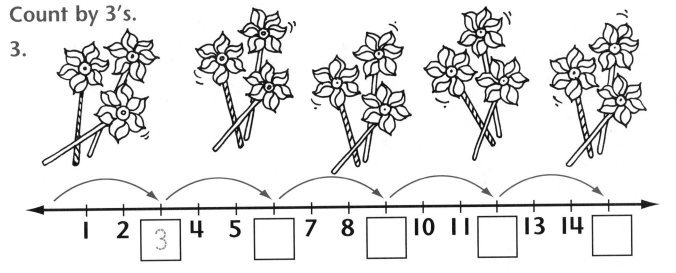

1 2 3 4 5 □ 7 8 □ 10 11 □ 13 14 □

4. 3, 6, _____ , _____ , 15, _____ , _____ , 24, 27, _____ ,

33, _____ , _____ , _____ , _____ ,48, _____ , _____ , _____ ,

60, _____ , 66, _____ , _____ , 75, _____ , _____ , _____

Count by 5's.

5.

5, 10, _15_, _____, _____, _____, 30, _____, _____, 45, _____,

_____, _____, 65, _____, _____, _____, 85, _____, _____

Count by 10's.

6.

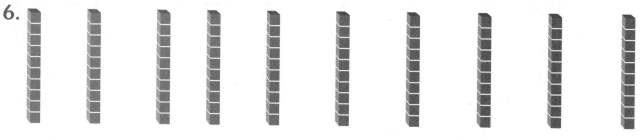

10, _____, _____, 40, _____, _____, _____, _____, _____, _____

Write the number.

1. 48 = ☐ tens and ☐ ones

☐ + ☐ = ☐

2. 53, _____, 55

Count by 2's.

3. _____, 14, _____, 18, 20, _____, _____

Name _____

Read the graph. Answer the questions.

Toy Shelf

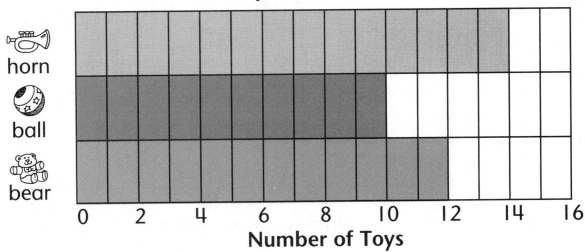

1. How many horns? _____

2. How many balls? _____

3. How many toy bears? _____

Complete the graph. Answer the questions.

Toy Store

doll

wagon

bicycle

Number of Toys

4. Show **8** dolls, **12** wagons, and **10** bicycles.

5. Are there more dolls than bicycles? _____

6. Are there fewer bicycles than wagons? _____

Unit 2 • Lesson 8

Complete the graph.

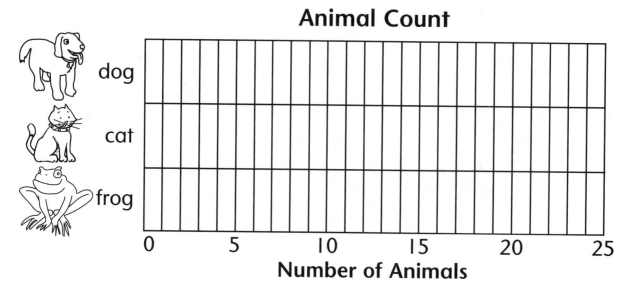

Animal Count

dog

cat

frog

0   5   10   15   20   25
Number of Animals

7. Show **25** dogs, **20** cats, and **10** frogs.

8. Are there more dogs than cats? How do you know?

★ **Test Prep**

Read the graph.
How many children in Room 5 like red? Mark your answer.

9

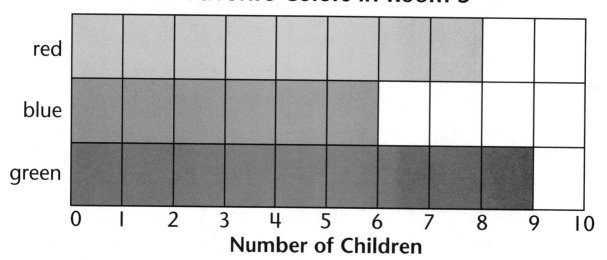

Favorite Colors in Room 5

red

blue

green

0   1   2   3   4   5   6   7   8   9   10
Number of Children

5 children   6 children   8 children   9 children
○   ○   ○   ○

52 (fifty-two)   Unit 2 • Lesson 8

Use the graph. Solve.

Favorite Sports

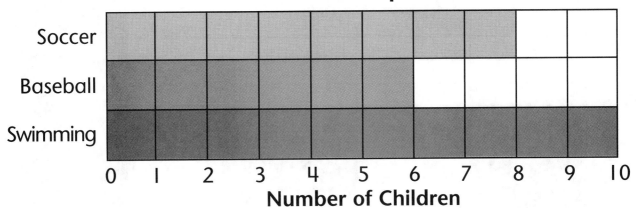

Number of Children

1. How many more children like soccer than baseball?

Think How many children like soccer?_____

How many children like baseball?_____

Do I add or subtract? _____

____ ◯ ____ = ____

Answer _____ more children like soccer.

- -

2. How many fewer children like baseball than swimming?

Think How many children like baseball? _____

How many children like swimming?_____

Do I add or subtract? _____

____ ◯ ____ = ____

Answer _____ fewer children like baseball.

- -

3. How many children like soccer or baseball?

Think How many children like soccer?_____

How many children like baseball?_____

Do I add or subtract? _____

____ ◯ ____ = ____

Answer _____ children like soccer or baseball.

Use the graph.

Think about whether you need to add or subtract. Solve.

Room 8 Bird Count

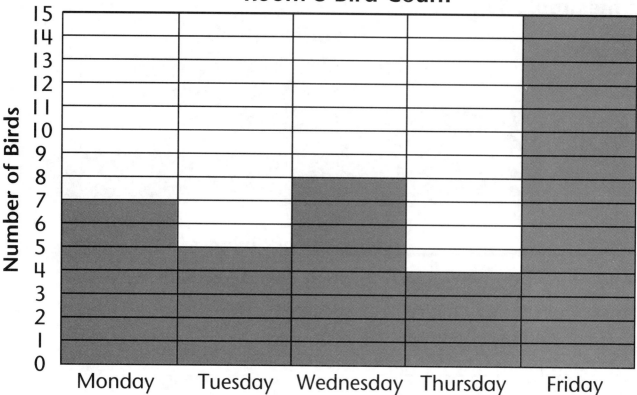

4. How many birds did Room 8 see on Monday and Tuesday?

   _____ ◯ _____ = _____

   Answer They saw _____ birds.

5. How many fewer birds did the class see on Thursday than on Wednesday?

   _____ ◯ _____ = _____

   Answer They saw _____ fewer birds on Thursday.

Extend Your Thinking

6. How does the bar graph help you compare the number of birds

   counted each day? _____

   _____

Complete.

1.
In **10¢** there is ____ dime.
In **10¢** there are __10__ pennies.

2.
In **20¢** there are ____ dimes.
In **20¢** there are ____ pennies.

3.
In **30¢** there are ____ dimes.
In **30¢** there are ____ pennies.

4.
In **40¢** there are ____ dimes.
In **40¢** there are ____ pennies.

Count by 10's. Write the amount. Use the ¢.

5.
__40¢__

6.
_____

7.
_____

8.
_____

Ring the correct answer.

9. **4** dimes are worth

(40¢) 50¢ 20¢

10. **I** dime is worth

50¢ 60¢ 10¢

11. **7** dimes are worth

20¢ 90¢ 70¢

12. **8** dimes are worth

50¢ 80¢ 90¢

Write the amount. Use the ¢. Do you see a pattern?

13. one dime ___10¢___   four dimes _____   seven dimes _____

two dimes _____   five dimes _____   eight dimes _____

three dimes _____   six dimes _____   nine dimes _____

Problem Solving
Reasoning Solve.

14. Shani has **3** dimes. Loni has **40¢**. Who has more money?

How do you know? _____

_____

_____

★ **Test Prep**

What is the value of the coins? Mark the space for your answer.

15

36¢   46¢   50¢   52¢
 ○   ○   ○   ○

Copyright © Houghton Mifflin Company. All rights reserved.

56 (fifty-six)

Unit 2 • Lesson 10

Name _____

Dime, Penny

Think of the dime as 1 ten.

Complete.

1.

dimes	pennies
2	5

25¢

2.

dimes	pennies

¢

3.

dimes	pennies

¢

4.

dime	pennies

¢

5.

dimes	pennies

¢

6.

dimes	pennies

¢

Unit 2 • Lesson 11

Complete.

7.　　**25** cents

dimes	pennies
2	5

25¢

8.　　**37** cents

dimes	pennies

37¢

9.　　**60** cents

dimes	pennies

60¢

Use > or < .

10.

70¢ (>) 30¢   41¢ ( ) 14¢   79¢ ( ) 97¢

Complete.

11. In **85¢** there are __8__ dimes and __5__ pennies.

12. In **70¢** there are ____ dimes and ____ pennies.

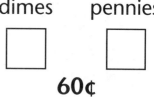
✓ Quick Check

Solve.

Favorite Fruit

Apples

Oranges

0　1　2　3　4　5　6
Number of Children

1. Read the graph.

   How many children like oranges?____

2. In **50¢** there are ____ dimes.

3. In **63¢** there are ____ dimes

   and ____ pennies.

58 (fifty-eight)

Unit 2 • Lesson 11

Ring the greatest number in each group.

1.	9	20	12
2.	85	90	57

3.	44	55	88
4.	90	93	89

Ring the least number in each group.

5.	9	7	6
6.	7	14	20

7.	12	91	94
8.	77	66	44

Use >, <, or =.

9. 10 ◯ 14   11. 12 ◯ 13   13. 63¢ ◯ 83¢   15. 76¢ ◯ 76¢

10. 11 ◯ 12   12. 16 ◯ 11   14. 91¢ ◯ 19¢   16. 46¢ ◯ 4¢

What comes

before?	between?	after?
17. _____ , 18	19. 16, _____ , 18	21. 16, _____
18. _____ , 27	20. 17, _____ , 19	22. 14, _____

Complete.

23.

	Tens	Ones
53		
19		
26		

24.

	Tens	Ones	
7	3		
9	9		
8	5		

Complete.

25. **2** tens and **3** ones = ☐ + ☐ = ☐

26. **8** tens and **6** ones = ☐ + ☐ = ☐

Count by 2's.

27.

10	12						24		

Count by 3's.

28.

3	6					24		

Match.

29. **8** dimes **5** pennies   **18¢**

30. **5** dimes **9** pennies   **59¢**

31. **1** dime **8** pennies   **85¢**

Problem Solving **Reasoning**	How many are there? Guess then check.

32.

guess _____   check _____

Unit 2 • Review

Name _____

1

○ 6 + 3 = 9   ○ 4 + 7 = 11

○ 10 − 5 = 5   ○ 10 − 4 = 6

2

7 = 12 − 5   14 > 6 + 6   13 − 8 > 14   2 + 9 < 13

   ○   ○   ○   ○

3

| 49 | | 51 |

47   48   50   52

○   ○   ○   ○

4

7 tens and **9** ones

77   79   85   97

○   ○   ○   ○

5

| 10 | 12 | 14 | | 18 | 20 |

13   15   16   22

○   ○   ○   ○

6

4 dimes   5 dimes   6 dimes   9 dimes

   ○   ○   ○   ○

Decide on an answer. Mark the space for your answer.
If the answer is **not here**, mark the space for **NH**.

7

$$\begin{array}{r} 7 \\ + \boxed{} \\ \hline 8 \end{array}$$

5	4	2	I	NH
○	○	○	○	○

8

$$\begin{array}{r} 5 \\ + 7 \\ \hline \boxed{} \end{array}$$

12	10	7	5	NH
○	○	○	○	○

9

$$\begin{array}{r} 6 \\ 3 \\ + 2 \\ \hline \boxed{} \end{array}$$

12	9	8	5	NH
○	○	○	○	○

10

$$\begin{array}{r} 3 \\ 3 \\ + 3 \\ \hline \boxed{} \end{array}$$

3	6	7	9	NH
○	○	○	○	○

62 (sixty-two)

Unit 2 • Cumulative Review

UNIT 3 • TABLE OF CONTENTS

Addition and Subtraction Facts through 20

UNIT 3 • TABLE OF CONTENTS

We will be using this vocabulary:

addend one of the numbers added in an addition problem

sum result of an addition problem

fact family related addition and subtraction facts

order property Changing the order of the addends does not change the sum.
$8 + 7 = 15; 7 + 8 = 15$

grouping property Changing the grouping of the addends does not change the sum.
$7 + (2 + 8) = 17; (7 + 2) + 8 = 17$

Dear Family,

During the next few weeks our math class will be learning and practicing addition and subtraction facts through 20. This is an extension of what we learned in Unit 1.

You can expect to see homework that provides practice with addition and subtraction facts.

As we learn about related facts and fact families, you may wish to keep the following sample as a guide.

Related Facts

$$9 + 8 = 17 \qquad 17 - 8 = 9$$

Fact Family

$$
\begin{array}{cccc}
7 & 9 & 16 & 16 \\
+\,9 & +\,7 & -\,9 & -\,7 \\
\hline
16 & 16 & 7 & 9 \\
\end{array}
$$

Knowing addition facts can help children learn the related subtraction facts.

Sincerely,

Name _____

Look at the picture and the facts.

$9 + 7 = 16$

$16 - 7 = 9$

Tell how they are related.

Complete. Then write a related addition or subtraction fact.

1.

$7 + 8 = \boxed{15}$

$15 - 8 = 7$

2.

$16 - 8 = \boxed{8}$

$8 + 8 = 16$

3.

$5 + 9 = \boxed{}$

_____

4.

$6 + 8 = \boxed{}$

_____

5.

$15 - 9 = \boxed{}$

_____

6.

$7 + 7 = \boxed{}$

_____

Unit 3 • Lesson 1

Complete. Then write a related addition or subtraction fact.

7.

$$\begin{array}{r} 8 \\ + 7 \\ \hline 15 \end{array} \qquad \begin{array}{r} 15 \\ - 7 \\ \hline 8 \end{array}$$

8.

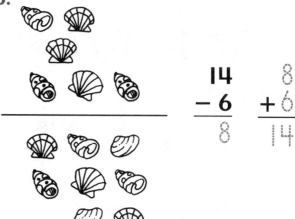

$$\begin{array}{r} 14 \\ - 6 \\ \hline 8 \end{array} \qquad \begin{array}{r} 8 \\ + 6 \\ \hline 14 \end{array}$$

9.

$$\begin{array}{r} 9 \\ + 7 \\ \hline \end{array} \qquad \begin{array}{r} \\ - \\ \hline \end{array}$$

10.

$$\begin{array}{r} 16 \\ - 8 \\ \hline \end{array} \qquad \begin{array}{r} \\ + \\ \hline \end{array}$$

11.

$$\begin{array}{r} 15 \\ - 9 \\ \hline \end{array} \qquad \begin{array}{r} \\ + \\ \hline \end{array}$$

12.

$$\begin{array}{r} 8 \\ + 8 \\ \hline \end{array} \qquad \begin{array}{r} \\ - \\ \hline \end{array}$$

13.

$$\begin{array}{r} 6 \\ + 9 \\ \hline \end{array} \qquad \begin{array}{r} \\ - \\ \hline \end{array}$$

14.

$$\begin{array}{r} 7 \\ + 9 \\ \hline \end{array} \qquad \begin{array}{r} \\ - \\ \hline \end{array}$$

15.

$$\begin{array}{r} 10 \\ + 4 \\ \hline \end{array} \qquad \begin{array}{r} \\ - \\ \hline \end{array}$$

16.

$$\begin{array}{r} 15 \\ - 8 \\ \hline \end{array} \qquad \begin{array}{r} \\ + \\ \hline \end{array}$$

17.

$$\begin{array}{r} 16 \\ - 9 \\ \hline \end{array} \qquad \begin{array}{r} \\ + \\ \hline \end{array}$$

Practice your facts. Complete.

18. $9 +$ ___ $= 15$

___ $+ 5 = 14$

___ $+ 7 = 14$

$4 +$ ___ $= 13$

___ $+ 8 = 15$

19. $16 = 9 +$ ___

$15 =$ ___ $+ 6$

$15 = 9 +$ ___

$16 =$ ___ $+ 7$

$14 = 8 +$ ___

20. $16 =$ ___ $+ 8$

___ $+ 7 = 15$

___ $+ 8 = 16$

$6 +$ ___ $= 15$

$9 +$ ___ $= 14$

Complete the names for the number.

21.  15 | $8 + \boxed{}$ | $6 + \boxed{}$ | $7 + \boxed{}$ | $9 + \boxed{}$

22.  16 | $9 + \boxed{}$ | $7 + \boxed{}$ | $8 + \boxed{}$ | $10 + \boxed{}$

23.  14 | $6 + \boxed{}$ | $7 + \boxed{}$ | $9 + \boxed{}$ | $8 + \boxed{}$

Use >, <, or =.

24. $13 \bigcirc 9 + 7$

$12 \bigcirc 6 + 5$

25. $16 \bigcirc 7 + 8$

$10 \bigcirc 4 + 5$

26. $8 \bigcirc 12 - 4$

$15 \bigcirc 8 + 4$

27. Gina has **15** shells.
She gives away **8** shells.
How many shells does
she have left?

___ ◯ ___ = ___

_____ shells

28. Arno has **8** blocks.
Lucy has **6** blocks.
How many blocks
do they have in all?

___ ◯ ___ = ___

_____ blocks

29. How many shells are there?
Guess then check.

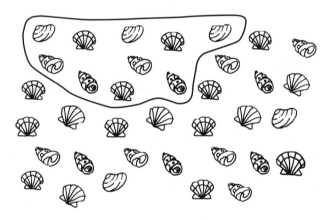

guess _____ check _____

30. How many blocks are there?
Guess then check.

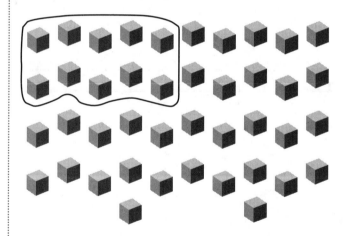

guess _____ check _____

★ **Test Prep**

Mark the related fact. Mark the space for your answer.

$9 + 7 = 16$

○ $16 - 7 = 9$ ○ $6 + 8 = 14$

○ $9 - 6 = 3$ ○ $8 + 7 = 15$

Name _____

Complete the fact family.

1.

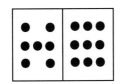

$7 + 9 = \boxed{16}$

$\underline{9} + \underline{7} = \boxed{16}$

$\underline{16} - \underline{9} = \boxed{7}$

$\underline{16} - \underline{7} = \boxed{9}$

2.

$\underline{8} + \underline{7} = \boxed{15}$

$\underline{} + \underline{} = \boxed{}$

$\underline{} - \underline{} = \boxed{}$

$\underline{} - \underline{} = \boxed{}$

3.

$7 + 6 = \boxed{}$

$\underline{} + \underline{} = \boxed{}$

$\underline{} - \underline{} = \boxed{}$

$\underline{} - \underline{} = \boxed{}$

4.

$9 + 6 = \boxed{}$

$\underline{} + \underline{} = \boxed{}$

$\underline{} - \underline{} = \boxed{}$

$\underline{} - \underline{} = \boxed{}$

5.

$4 + 9 = \boxed{}$

$\underline{} + \underline{} = \boxed{}$

$\underline{} - \underline{} = \boxed{}$

$\underline{} - \underline{} = \boxed{}$

6.

$6 + 6 = \boxed{}$

$\underline{} - \underline{} = \boxed{}$

Unit 3 • Lesson 2

Write the fact family.

7.   **7, 9, 16**

$$\begin{array}{r} 7 \\ + 9 \\ \hline 16 \end{array} \quad \begin{array}{r} 9 \\ + 7 \\ \hline 16 \end{array} \quad \begin{array}{r} 16 \\ - 9 \\ \hline 7 \end{array} \quad \begin{array}{r} 16 \\ - 7 \\ \hline 9 \end{array}$$

8.   **6, 8, 14**

$$\begin{array}{r} 6 \\ + 8 \\ \hline \end{array} \quad +\underline{} \quad -\underline{} \quad -\underline{}$$

9.   **9, 5, 14**

$$+\underline{} \quad +\underline{} \quad -\underline{} \quad -\underline{}$$

10.   **7, 7, 14**

$$+\underline{} \quad -\underline{}$$

Problem Solving Reasoning

11. Why are there only two facts for the fact family in exercise 10?

_____

_____

_____

★ Test Prep

Which of these completes the fact family? Mark the space for your answer.

$$8 + 8 = 16$$

○ $8 + 7 = 15$ ○ $16 - 8 = 8$

○ $6 + 8 = 14$ ○ $16 - 9 = 7$

Unit 3 • Lesson 2

Solve.

1. There are **15** cows.
   There is **1** hen.
   6 cows are black.
   How many cows are
   not black?

   Think Is there too much
   information?
   I will ring what I do not need.

   ____ ◯ ____ = ☐

   Answer ____ cows

2. There are **6** horses in the barn.
   There are **3** cows.
   There are **8** horses in the field.
   How many horses are there in
   all?

   Think Is there too much
   information?
   I will ring what I do not need.

   ____ ◯ ____ = ☐

   Answer ____ horses

Ring the information you do not need.
Solve.

3. There are **15** chickens.
   7 chickens are white.
   6 cats are black.
   How many chickens are not white?

   Answer ____ chickens

4. There are **8** baskets of white eggs.
   There are **8** baskets of brown eggs.
   José saw **3** birds.
   How many baskets of eggs are there?

   Answer _____ baskets of eggs

5. There are **9** big ducks.
   There are **5** little ducks.
   There are **7** little pigs.
   How many ducks are there in all?

   ___ ◯ ___ = ☐

   Answer _____ ducks

6. There are **16** horses.
   8 chickens are white.
   7 horses run away.
   How many horses are left?

   Answer ____ horses

Extend Your Thinking

7. How do you know your answer to exercise 6 is correct?
   Draw or write to explain.

```



```

72 (seventy-two)

Unit 3 • Lesson 3

Name _____

How does knowing the addition fact help you remember the subtraction fact?

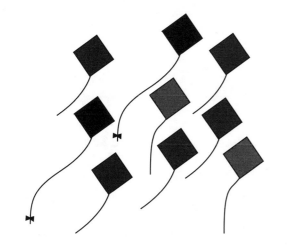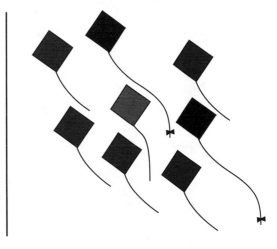

$$9 + 8 = 17$$

$$17 - 8 = ?$$

Complete. Then write a related addition or subtraction fact.

1.
$$16 - 9 = \boxed{7}$$

$$\underline{7 + 9 = 16}$$

2.
$$7 + 9 = \boxed{}$$

_____

3.
$$8 + 8 = \boxed{}$$

_____

4.
$$17 - 9 = \boxed{}$$

_____

5.
$$15 - 8 = \boxed{}$$

_____

6.
$$6 + 9 = \boxed{}$$

_____

Complete. Then write a related addition or subtraction fact.

7.

$$\begin{array}{r} 7 \\ +\,8 \\ \hline 15 \end{array} \qquad \begin{array}{r} 15 \\ -\,8 \\ \hline 7 \end{array}$$

8.

$$\begin{array}{r} 17 \\ -\,8 \\ \hline 9 \end{array} \qquad \begin{array}{r} 9 \\ +\,8 \\ \hline 17 \end{array}$$

9.

$$\begin{array}{r} 7 \\ +\,9 \\ \hline \end{array} \qquad -\,\rule{1cm}{0.4pt}$$

10.

$$\begin{array}{r} 9 \\ +\,9 \\ \hline \end{array} \qquad -\,\rule{1cm}{0.4pt}$$

11.

$$\begin{array}{r} 16 \\ -\,8 \\ \hline \end{array} \qquad +\,\rule{1cm}{0.4pt}$$

12.

$$\begin{array}{r} 15 \\ -\,8 \\ \hline \end{array} \qquad +\,\rule{1cm}{0.4pt}$$

13.

$$\begin{array}{r} 13 \\ -\,7 \\ \hline \end{array} \qquad +\,\rule{1cm}{0.4pt}$$

14.

$$\begin{array}{r} 9 \\ +\,6 \\ \hline \end{array} \qquad -\,\rule{1cm}{0.4pt}$$

Practice your facts. Complete.

15. $9 + \underline{\hspace{1cm}} = 16$

$\underline{\hspace{1cm}} + 8 = 18$

$9 + \underline{\hspace{1cm}} = 14$

16. $15 = 9 + \underline{\hspace{1cm}}$

$15 = \underline{\hspace{1cm}} + 6$

$18 = \underline{\hspace{1cm}} + 9$

17. $\boxed{} = 7 + 7$

$\boxed{} = 5 + 8$

$14 = \underline{\hspace{1cm}} + 5$

Write the missing addends.

18.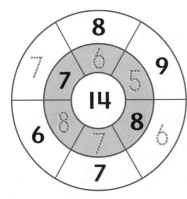

19.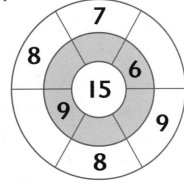

20.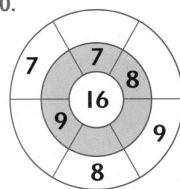

Use >, <, or =.

21. 4 + 7 ◯ 12

8 + 5 ◯ 13

10 − 7 ◯ 11

22. 16 − 9 ◯ 8

15 − 8 ◯ 5

9 + 9 ◯ 17

23. 8 + 6 ◯ 14

14 − 8 ◯ 6

7 + 6 ◯ 17

| **Problem Solving Reasoning** | **Choose the operation. Solve.** |

24. Kodia has **17** balloons. She gives Dawn **9** balloons. How many balloons does Kodia have now?

____ ◯ ____ = ____

____ balloons

25. Aaron sees **8** blue kites in the sky. Jody sees **8** red kites in the sky. How many kites do Aaron and Jody see together?

____ ◯ ____ = ____

____ kites

Do you need all the information? Ring what you do not need. Solve.

26. There are **6** kites with long tails. There are **9** kites with short tails.
The kites are high in the sky. How many kites are there in all?

____ ◯ ____ = ____

_____ kites

27. Pablo sees **4** kites.
He sees **17** balloons.
9 balloons pop.
How many balloons does he see now?

____ ◯ ____ = ____

____ balloons

✔ Quick Check

Complete. Match the related fact.

1. $18 - 9 = 9$ $9 + 8 = \square$

   $16 - 8 = 8$ $16 - 9 = \square$

   $7 + 9 = 16$ $8 + 8 = \square$

   $17 - 8 = 9$ $9 + 9 = \square$

Complete the fact family.

2.   7
      + 8   +___   −___   −___

3.   9
      + 8   +___   −___   −___

Name _____

Complete the fact family.

1.

$9 + 8 = 17$

$8 + 9 = 17$

$17 - 8 = 9$

$17 - 9 = 8$

2.

$6 + 8 = \boxed{}$

$\text{\underline{}} + \text{\underline{}} = \boxed{}$

$\text{\underline{}} - \text{\underline{}} = \boxed{}$

$\text{\underline{}} - \text{\underline{}} = \boxed{}$

3.

$9 + 7 = \boxed{}$

$\text{\underline{}} + \text{\underline{}} = \boxed{}$

$\text{\underline{}} - \text{\underline{}} = \boxed{}$

$\text{\underline{}} - \text{\underline{}} = \boxed{}$

4.

$8 + 8 = \boxed{}$

$\text{\underline{}} - \text{\underline{}} = \boxed{}$

5.

$9 + 6 = \boxed{}$

$\text{\underline{}} + \text{\underline{}} = \boxed{}$

$\text{\underline{}} - \text{\underline{}} = \boxed{}$

$\text{\underline{}} - \text{\underline{}} = \boxed{}$

6.

$8 + 7 = \boxed{}$

$\text{\underline{}} + \text{\underline{}} = \boxed{}$

$\text{\underline{}} - \text{\underline{}} = \boxed{}$

$\text{\underline{}} - \text{\underline{}} = \boxed{}$

Unit 3 • Lesson 5

Write the fact family.

7.   **8, 9, 17**

$$\begin{array}{r} 8 \\ +\,9 \\ \hline 17 \end{array} \qquad \begin{array}{r} 9 \\ +\,8 \\ \hline 17 \end{array} \qquad \begin{array}{r} 17 \\ -\,9 \\ \hline 8 \end{array} \qquad \begin{array}{r} 17 \\ -\,8 \\ \hline 9 \end{array}$$

8.   **9, 9, 18**

$$\begin{array}{r} 9 \\ +\,9 \\ \hline \end{array} \qquad \begin{array}{r} \\ -\, \\ \hline \end{array}$$

9.   **9, 8, 17**

$$\begin{array}{r} + \\ \hline \end{array} \qquad \begin{array}{r} + \\ \hline \end{array} \qquad \begin{array}{r} - \\ \hline \end{array} \qquad \begin{array}{r} - \\ \hline \end{array}$$

10.   **6, 9, 15**

$$\begin{array}{r} + \\ \hline \end{array} \qquad \begin{array}{r} + \\ \hline \end{array} \qquad \begin{array}{r} - \\ \hline \end{array} \qquad \begin{array}{r} - \\ \hline \end{array}$$

11.   **4, 9, 13**

$$\begin{array}{r} + \\ \hline \end{array} \qquad \begin{array}{r} + \\ \hline \end{array} \qquad \begin{array}{r} - \\ \hline \end{array} \qquad \begin{array}{r} - \\ \hline \end{array}$$

12.   **8, 6, 14**

$$\begin{array}{r} + \\ \hline \end{array} \qquad \begin{array}{r} + \\ \hline \end{array} \qquad \begin{array}{r} - \\ \hline \end{array} \qquad \begin{array}{r} - \\ \hline \end{array}$$

★ Test Prep

Which number sentence belongs to the fact family?
Mark the space next to your answer.

9, 7, 16

  ○ 16 − 8 = 8   ○ 7 + 8 = 15

  ○ 16 − 7 = 9   ○ 9 + 8 = 17

       Unit 3 • Lesson 5

Complete. Then write the fact another way.

1. $5 + 8 = \boxed{13}$

    $\underline{8} + \underline{5} = 13$

2. $9 + 8 = \boxed{}$

    ___ + ___ = 17

3. $6 + 9 = \boxed{}$

    ___ + ___ = $\boxed{}$

4. $4 + 9 = \boxed{}$

    ___ + ___ = $\boxed{}$

5. $8 + 7 = \boxed{}$

    ___ + ___ = $\boxed{}$

6. $7 + 9 = \boxed{}$

    ___ + ___ = $\boxed{}$

7. $6 + 8 = \boxed{}$

    ___ + ___ = $\boxed{}$

8. $9 + 5 = \boxed{}$

    ___ + ___ = $\boxed{}$

Complete the number sentence.

9. $(7 + 2) + 8 =$

    $\underline{9} + 8 = \boxed{}$

10. $9 + (3 + 6) =$

    ___ + ___ = $\boxed{}$

11. $6 + (4 + 5) =$

    ___ + ___ = $\boxed{}$

12. $8 + (4 + 2) =$

    ___ + ___ = $\boxed{}$

13. $3 + (5 + 4) =$

    ___ + ___ = $\boxed{}$

14. $7 + (5 + 4) =$

    ___ + ___ = $\boxed{}$

Complete. Then write the fact another way.

15.
```
    9        8
  + 8      + 9
   17       17
```

16.
```
    7        9
  + 9      + □
```

17.
```
    6
  + 8      +
                14
```

18.
```
    6
  + 7      +
   13
```

19.
```
    7
  + 8      +
```

20.
```
    9
  + □      +
   12
```

Group. Then find the sums.

21.
```
   3 ⟩ 7      5        8        6        4        3
   4            4        1        3        5        6
 + 7          + 7      + 4      + 7      + 6      + 8
```

Problem Solving
Reasoning

22. Show how you would group 4 + 6 + 8 = □ to add.

Explain why. _____

_____

★ Test Prep

23 Solve. Mark your answer.

$$8 + 5 + 2 = \boxed{}$$

| 19 | 18 | 15 | 12 |
| ○ | ○ | ○ | ○ |

Name _____

Complete the tables.

1. Add 5.

9	14
4	
8	
6	
7	

2. Add 6.

8	
10	
7	
5	
9	

3. Add 8.

7	
5	
8	
9	
6	

4. Subtract 9.

17	8
15	
18	
14	
12	

5. Subtract 8.

15	
13	
12	
17	
14	

6. Subtract 7.

16	
14	
12	
9	
13	

Complete the rule.

7. Subtract 5.

14	9
8	3
12	7
11	6
13	8

8. Add ____.

7	14
9	16
5	12
8	15
4	11

9. Subtract ____.

14	8
11	5
15	9
10	4
13	7

Solve.

10. $6 + \boxed{} = 14$

11. $8 + \boxed{} = 15$

12. $5 + \boxed{} = 12$

13. $9 + \boxed{} = 17$

Problem Solving Reasoning Solve.

14. Andy finds **16** frogs before and after school.
He finds **7** frogs before school.
How many frogs does he find after school?

_____ frogs

 Quick Check

Write the fact family.

1. **9, 8, 17**

$+$ ___ $+$ ___ $-$ ___ $-$ ___

Solve.

2.   6
     3
   $+\ 7$
   _____

Complete the rule.

3. **Add _____.**

4	13
9	18
6	15
2	11

Name _____

Solve.

1. $10 + 1 = \boxed{11}$

2. $11 - 1 = \boxed{10}$

 $10 + 2 = \boxed{}$

$12 - 2 = \boxed{}$

 $10 + 3 = \boxed{}$

$13 - 3 = \boxed{}$

$10 + 4 = \boxed{}$

$14 - 4 = \boxed{}$

$10 + 5 = \boxed{}$

$15 - 5 = \boxed{}$

**Problem Solving
Reasoning**

3. What pattern do you see in exercise 2? _____

_____

Solve.

4. $20 - 10 = \boxed{10}$

         $19 - 10 = \boxed{}$

         $18 - 10 = \boxed{}$

         $17 - 10 = \boxed{}$

         $16 - 10 = \boxed{}$

         $15 - 10 = \boxed{}$

5. $10 + 10 = \boxed{20}$

         $9 + 10 = \boxed{}$

         $8 + 10 = \boxed{}$

         $7 + 10 = \boxed{}$

         $6 + 10 = \boxed{}$

         $5 + 10 = \boxed{}$

Problem Solving Reasoning   Look at exercises 4 and 5.
Continue the patterns.

6. $\underline{14} - \underline{10} = \boxed{4}$

       $\underline{} - \underline{} = \boxed{}$

       $\underline{} - \underline{} = \boxed{}$

       $\underline{} - \underline{} = \boxed{}$

7. $\underline{4} + \underline{10} = \boxed{14}$

       $\underline{} + \underline{} = \boxed{}$

       $\underline{} + \underline{} = \boxed{}$

       $\underline{} + \underline{} = \boxed{}$

★ Test Prep

8 Solve. Mark the space under your answer.

$10 + \boxed{} = 19$

0	5	9	10
○	○	○	○

9

$13 - \boxed{} = 10$

0	3	5	6
○	○	○	○

Name _____

Problem

Julian sees **17** birds.
9 of the birds are red.
How many birds are not red?

1 **Understand**

I need to find out how many birds are not red.

2 **Decide**

I can write a number sentence to solve the problem.

3 **Solve**

$17 - 9 = \underline{8}$

There are __8__ birds that are not red.

4 **Look back**

My answer makes sense
because $9 + 8 = 17$.

Write a number sentence. Solve.

1. **7** children have big dogs.
   9 children have little dogs.
   How many children have dogs?

   _____ children

Write a number sentence. Solve.

2. There are **12** dogs
   on the porch.
   There are **9** cats
   in the tree.
   How many more dogs
   are there than cats?

   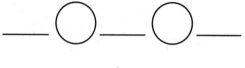

   _____ more dogs

3. There are **8** puppies
   in the yard.
   7 more puppies come.
   How many puppies are
   there now?

   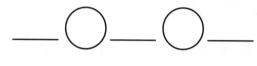

   _____ puppies

4. There are **18** birds on the fence.
   9 fly away. How many are left?

   _____ birds

5. **4** red birds fly away.
   4 blue birds fly away.
   9 brown birds fly away. How many birds fly away?

      _____ birds

Write a story to go with the number sentence.

6. **9 + 8 = 17** _____

   _____

   _____

Complete. Then write a related addition or subtraction fact.

1. $9 + 8 = \boxed{}$ 2. $20 - 10 = \boxed{}$ 3. $18 - 9 = \boxed{}$

_____   _____   _____

Write the fact family.

4. 6, 8, 14

$+$ ___ $+$ ___ $-$ ___ $-$ ___

5. 8, 7, 15

$+$ ___ $+$ ___ $-$ ___ $-$ ___

6. 9, 7, 16

$+$ ___ $+$ ___ $-$ ___ $-$ ___

7. 9, 9, 18

$+$ ___ $-$ ___

Solve.

8. $5 + \boxed{} = 13$ 9. $7 + \boxed{} = 14$ 10. $8 + \boxed{} = 12$

11.
$$\begin{array}{r} 10 \\ + \boxed{} \\ \hline 18 \end{array}$$

12.
$$\begin{array}{r} 8 \\ + \boxed{} \\ \hline 17 \end{array}$$

13.
$$\begin{array}{r} 5 \\ + \boxed{} \\ \hline 14 \end{array}$$

14.
$$\begin{array}{r} 7 \\ + \boxed{} \\ \hline 13 \end{array}$$

Use + or −.

15.
16 ⃝ 9
———
7

16.
8 ⃝ 5
———
13

17.
15 ⃝ 8
———
7

18.
8 ⃝ 4
———
4

Use >, <, or =.

19. 14 ◯ 17

20. 8 + 6 ◯ 12

21. 9 ◯ 9 + 2

22. 6+ 7 ◯ 13

23. 15 − 9 ◯ 6

24. 17 ◯ 11 − 5

Add.

25.
  6
  6
+ 6
———

26.
  5
  6
+ 7
———

27.
  7
  3
+ 9
———

28.
  8
  4
+ 4
———

| **Problem Solving** | Write the number sentence. Solve. |
| **Reasoning** | |

29. Peg has **5** red hats, **4** blue hats, and **6** green hats.
How many hats does she have in all?

____ ◯ ____ ◯ ____ ◯ ____   _____ hats

30. Sal sees **17** birds. **8** birds are on the fence.
How many birds are not on the fence?

____ ◯ ____ ◯ ____   _____ birds

88 (eighty-eight)

Unit 3 • Review

1

19 < 16	10 < 8	13 = 11	13 > 9
○	○	○	○

2

77	79	87	97
○	○	○	○

3

9, 8, 17 | ○ 16 − 8 = 8   ○ 9 + 7 = 16

○ 17 − 8 = 9   ○ 8 + 7 = 15

4

13 animals	15 animals	17 animals	19 animals
○	○	○	○

5

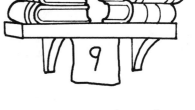

7 more books
○

9 more books
○

8 more books
○

10 more books
○

6

$7 + 6 = 13$
○

$7 + 9 = 16$
○

$13 - 7 = 6$
○

$16 - 9 = 7$
○

Decide on an answer. Mark the space for your answer.
If the answer is **not here**, mark the space for **NH**.

7

$8 + 9 = \square$

15	16	17	18	NH
○	○	○	○	○

8

Tens	Ones
8	2

89	82	68	28	NH
○	○	○	○	○

9

$9 + (3 + 5) = \square$

19	18	17	16	NH
○	○	○	○	○

10

$6 + 7 \bigcirc 9 + 3$

<	>	=	NH
○	○	○	○

Copyright © Houghton Mifflin Company. All rights reserved.

Unit 3 • Cumulative Review

UNIT 4 • TABLE OF CONTENTS

Geometry and Fractions

Dear Family,

During the next few weeks our math class will be learning about geometry and fractions.

You can expect to see homework that provides practice with geometric solids and plane figures. There will also be homework that provides practice with fractions.

As we learn about geometry and fractions, you may wish to keep the following sample as a guide.

Geometric Solids

Cone   Cube   Cylinder   Rectangular Prism   Square Pyramid   Sphere

Plane Figures

Square   Rectangle   Triangle   Circle

Fractions

$\dfrac{1}{3}$ $\dfrac{1}{4}$ $\dfrac{1}{2}$

Sincerely,

Name _____   **Solids**

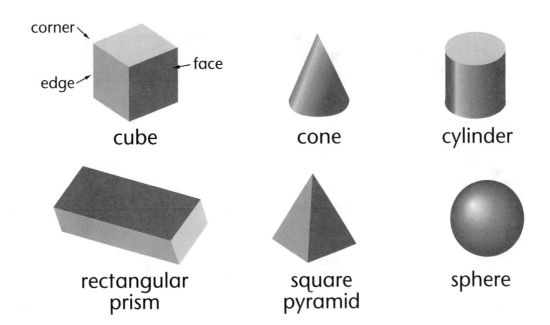

corner

edge   face

cube   cone   cylinder

rectangular   square   sphere
prism   pyramid

Look at the solids.
Write how many faces, edges, and corners.

	Name of Solid	Number of Flat Faces	Number of Edges	Number of Corners
1.	cube	6	12	8
2.	rectangular prism			
3.	square pyramid			
4.	sphere			

Complete the table.

		Slides	Stacks	Rolls
5.		yes	no	yes
6.				
7.				
8.				
9.				

Problem Solving Reasoning

10. How are a cone and a cylinder alike? How are they different?

_____

_____

_____

_____

★ Test Prep

Mark the cube.

94 (ninety-four)

Unit 4 • Lesson 1

Name _____

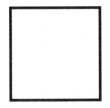 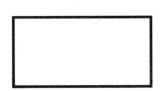  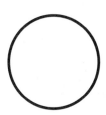

| Square | Rectangle | Triangle | Circle |

Find a solid that matches the picture.
Trace around the solid to make a plane figure.
What plane figure did you draw? Write the name.

1.

circle
_____

2.

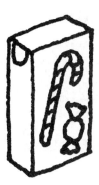

_____

3.

_____

4.

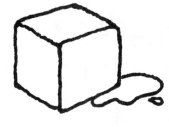

_____

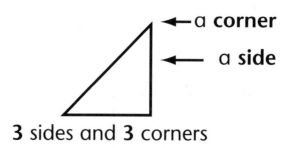

← a corner

← a side

3 sides and 3 corners

How many sides?
How many corners?

5.

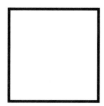

__4__ sides

__4__ corners

6.

____ sides

____ corners

7.

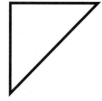

____ sides

____ corners

8.

____ sides

____ corners

9.

____ sides

____ corners

10.

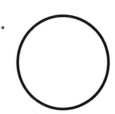

____ sides

____ corners

Mark what figure you will see if you trace the face of the solid.

11

  | ○   ○ ○   ○

Name _____

These two figures are **congruent**. They are the same size and the same shape.

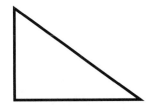 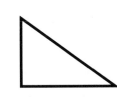

These two figures are not congruent. They are the same shape but not the same size.

Ring the figure that is congruent to the first figure.

1.  |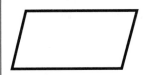

2. |

3. 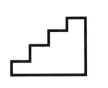 |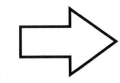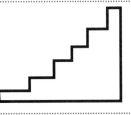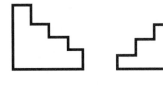

4. 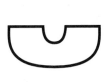 |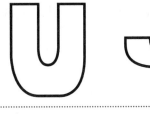

5. |

This figure is **symmetrical**.

Both parts match.

This figure is not symmetrical.

Both parts do not match.

Ring the figures that are symmetrical.

6.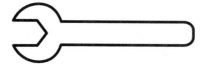

 Quick Check

cube

Look at the picture. Answer the questions.

1. How many faces? _____ faces

   How many edges? _____ edges

   How many corners? _____ corners

Name the figure that is the face of the cube.

2. _____

Ring the symmetrical figures.

3.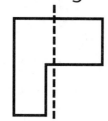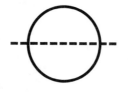

Name _____

Problem

Draw a line to make the rectangle into **2** squares.

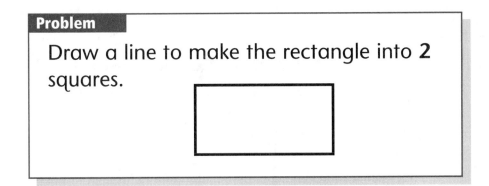

1 **Understand**

I need to draw a line to make the rectangle into **2** squares.

2 **Decide**

I can draw lines on the picture of the rectangle until I find the line that makes **2** squares.

3 **Solve**

First Try   Second Try

4 **Look back**

My second try was correct.
I know because a square has **4** sides and all the sides are the same length.

Draw a picture to solve.

1. Draw a line to make the square into **2** rectangles.

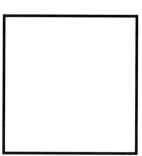

2. Draw **3** lines to make the hexagon into **6** triangles.

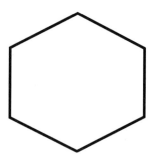

3. Draw **2** lines to make the trapezoid into **3** triangles.

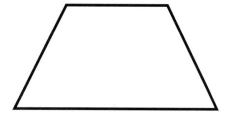

4. Draw a line to make the rectangle into **2** triangles.

5. Cut out a rectangle, a square, and a triangle. Then cut each figure to make **2** new figures. Draw the new figures.

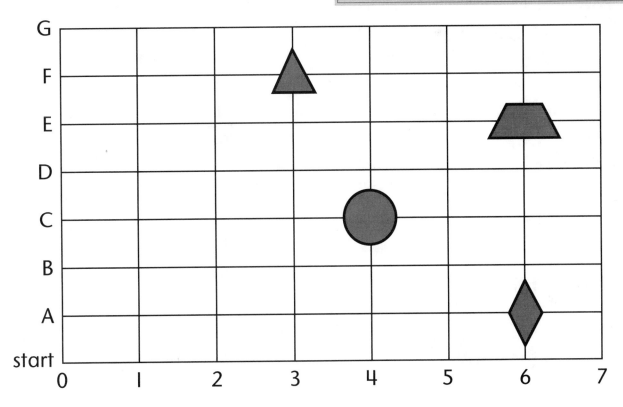

Use the picture. Solve.

1. Where is the ▲ ?
   Think Find the figure.
   Follow the line down.
   Follow the line across.

   Answer _3, F_

2. Where is the ● ?
   Think Find the figure.
   Follow the line down.
   Follow the line across.

   Answer _____

3. Where is the ⬭ ?
   Think Find the figure.
   Follow the line down.
   Follow the line across.

   Answer _____

4. Where is the ◆ ?
   Think Find the figure.
   Follow the line down.
   Follow the line across.

   Answer _____

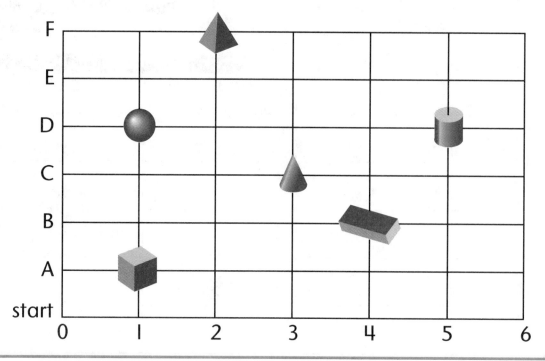

Use the picture. Solve.

5. Where is the ?

Answer _____

6. Where is the ?

Answer _____

7. Where is the ?

Answer _____

8. Where is the ?

Answer _____

9. Where is the ?

Answer _____

10. Where is the ?

Answer _____

Use the picture. Follow the direction.

11. Draw a square at 4, E.

We call $\frac{1}{2}$, $\frac{1}{3}$, and $\frac{1}{4}$ fractions.

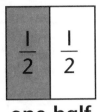

| one half | one third | one fourth |

Here are some other fractions.

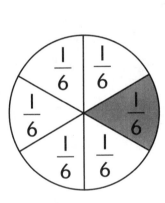

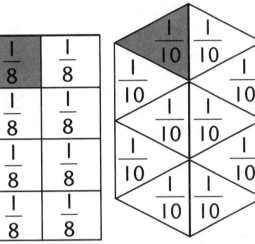

one fifth   one sixth   one eighth   one tenth   one twelfth

Color one part. Ring the correct fraction.

I.

$\frac{1}{2}$ or $\frac{1}{4}$

2.

$\frac{1}{3}$ or $\frac{1}{4}$

3.

$\frac{1}{2}$ or $\frac{1}{3}$

4.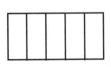

$\frac{1}{5}$ or $\frac{1}{6}$

5.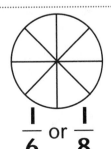

$\frac{1}{6}$ or $\frac{1}{8}$

6.

$\frac{1}{6}$ or $\frac{1}{10}$

Write the fraction in each part.

7.

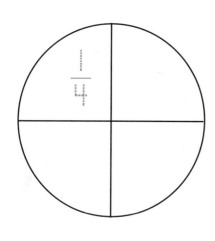

8.

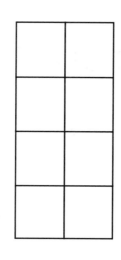

9.

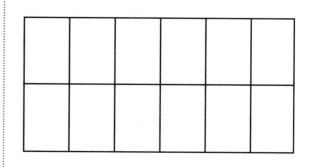

10.

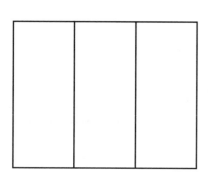

11.

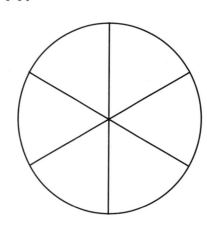

12.

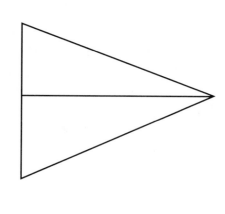

Problem Solving
Reasoning

13. Which is greater, $\dfrac{1}{6}$ or $\dfrac{1}{12}$ of a whole? Why? _____

_____

★ Test Prep

Mark the correct fraction.

 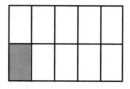

$\dfrac{1}{5}$ $\dfrac{1}{8}$ $\dfrac{1}{10}$ $\dfrac{1}{12}$

○   ○   ○   ○

     Unit 4 • Lesson 6

This figure has **8** equal parts.
5 of the **8** parts are colored.

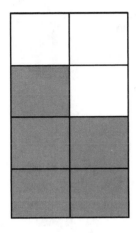

5	colored parts
8	equal parts

$\frac{5}{8}$ of the figure is colored.

Five eighths is colored.

Color to show the fraction.
Write the fraction.

1. two fifths

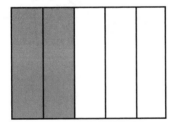

$\frac{2}{5}$

2. three tenths

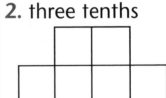

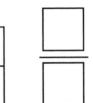

3. four ninths

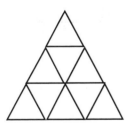

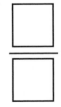

4. six sixths

5. If $\frac{4}{4}$ equals **1** or the whole, then what does $\frac{3}{3}$ equal?

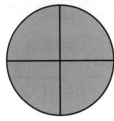 

_____

Ring the fraction that shows what part is colored.

6.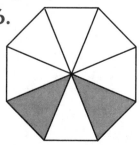

$\dfrac{6}{8}$ $\left(\dfrac{2}{8}\right)$ $\dfrac{1}{6}$

7.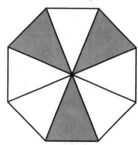

$\dfrac{3}{6}$ $\dfrac{5}{8}$ $\dfrac{3}{8}$

8.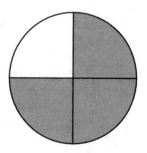

$\dfrac{3}{4}$ $\dfrac{2}{3}$ $\dfrac{1}{4}$

Ring the fraction that shows what part is not colored.

9.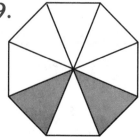

$\left(\dfrac{6}{8}\right)$ $\dfrac{2}{8}$ $\dfrac{1}{6}$

10.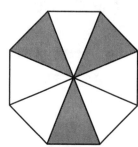

$\dfrac{3}{6}$ $\dfrac{5}{8}$ $\dfrac{3}{8}$

11.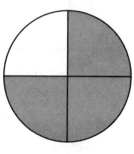

$\dfrac{3}{4}$ $\dfrac{2}{3}$ $\dfrac{1}{4}$

Problem Solving
Reasoning

12. Is $\dfrac{2}{4}$ greater than, less than, or equal to $\dfrac{1}{2}$? _____

Draw a picture to show why.

★ Test Prep

Mark under the fraction that shows what part is colored.

13.

$\dfrac{1}{2}$ $\dfrac{3}{5}$ $\dfrac{2}{5}$ $\dfrac{1}{10}$

○   ○   ○   ○

106 (one hundred six)

Unit 4 • Lesson 7

Name _____

Ring $\frac{1}{2}$ of the set. Complete.

1.

$\frac{1}{2}$ of 8 = __4__

2.

$\frac{1}{2}$ of 10 = ____

3.

$\frac{1}{2}$ of 14 = ____

4.

$\frac{1}{2}$ of 12 = ____

Ring $\frac{1}{4}$ of the set. Complete.

5.

$\frac{1}{4}$ of 12 = __3__

6.

$\frac{1}{4}$ of 4 = ____

7.

$\frac{1}{4}$ of 16 = ____

8.

$\frac{1}{4}$ of 8 = ____

Unit 4 • Lesson 8

Ring $\frac{3}{4}$ of the set. Complete.

9.

$\frac{3}{4}$ of 4 = ___3___

10.

$\frac{3}{4}$ of 12 = _____

Ring $\frac{2}{3}$ of the set. Complete.

11.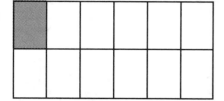

$\frac{2}{3}$ of 9 = _____

12.

$\frac{2}{3}$ of 15 = _____

☑ Quick Check

Write the fraction for the colored part.

1.

2.

Ring $\frac{2}{3}$ of the set. Complete.

3.  $\frac{2}{3}$ of 12 = _____

Match.

1. cone

2. cube

3. square
   pyramid

Look at the solids.
Complete the table.

Solid	Number of Flat Faces	Stacks	Rolls
4.			
5.			
6.			

Write how many sides and corners.

7. ____ sides

   ____ corners

8. ____ sides

   ____ corners

9. ____ sides

   ____ corners

Ring the figure that is congruent to the first figure.

10.

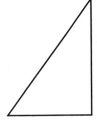

Color one part.
Ring the correct fraction.

11.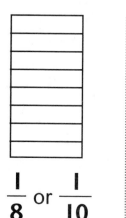

$\dfrac{1}{8}$ or $\dfrac{1}{10}$

12.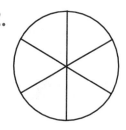

$\dfrac{1}{6}$ or $\dfrac{1}{8}$

13.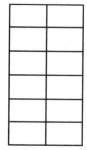

$\dfrac{1}{10}$ or $\dfrac{1}{12}$

14.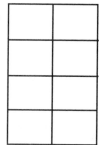

$\dfrac{1}{6}$ or $\dfrac{1}{8}$

Ring the fraction that shows what part is colored.

15.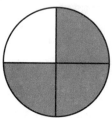

$\dfrac{1}{4}$ $\dfrac{2}{3}$ $\dfrac{3}{4}$

16.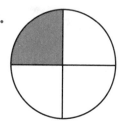

$\dfrac{1}{4}$ $\dfrac{2}{3}$ $\dfrac{3}{4}$

17.

$\dfrac{4}{5}$ $\dfrac{3}{5}$ $\dfrac{5}{10}$

18.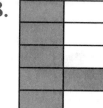

$\dfrac{6}{10}$ $\dfrac{4}{10}$ $\dfrac{2}{5}$

Ring $\dfrac{2}{3}$ of the set. Complete.

19. ✖ ✖ ✖ ✖ ✖
✖ ✖ ✖ ✖ ✖
✖ ✖ ✖ ✖ ✖

$\dfrac{2}{3}$ of 15 = _____

20. ⚪ ⚪ ⚪
⚪ ⚪ ⚪
⚪ ⚪ ⚪

$\dfrac{2}{3}$ of 9 = _____

Problem Solving Reasoning Use the picture. Solve.

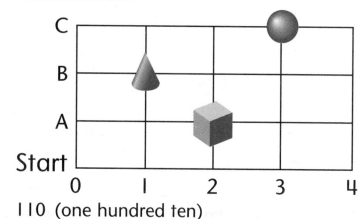

21. Where is the cube? _____

22. Where is the sphere? _____

23. Where is the cone? _____

110 (one hundred ten)

Unit 4 • Review

Name_____

1

78		80

77　　79　　81　　87
○　　○　　○　　○

2

21	24	27		33	36

26　　28　　30　　39
○　　○　　○　　○

3

$9 + 8 = 17$

○ $17 - 9 = 8$　　　○ $8 + 7 = 15$

○ $7 + 9 = 16$　　　○ $16 - 9 = 7$

4

$7 + 7 = 14$　　$7 + 8 = 15$　　　$14 - 7 = 7$　　　$14 - 5 = 9$
○　　　　　　○　　　　　　　○　　　　　　　○

5

　　　　○　　
○　　　　　　○　　　　　　　　　　　　　○

6

 ○    ○    ○    ○

7

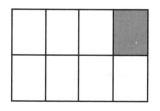

$\dfrac{1}{4}$ ○ $\dfrac{1}{8}$ ○ $\dfrac{1}{10}$ ○ $\dfrac{1}{12}$ ○

8

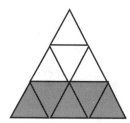

$\dfrac{1}{9}$ ○ $\dfrac{4}{9}$ ○ $\dfrac{5}{9}$ ○ $\dfrac{9}{9}$ ○

9

 $\dfrac{1}{4}$ of 12 = ____

3 ○   4 ○   9 ○   12 ○

10

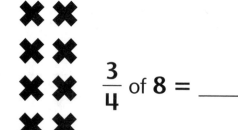 $\dfrac{3}{4}$ of 8 = ____

3 ○   4 ○   6 ○   8 ○

Unit 4 • Cumulative Review

UNIT 5 • TABLE OF CONTENTS

Measurement

UNIT 5 • TABLE OF CONTENTS

(one hundred thirteen) 113

We will be using this vocabulary:

kilogram a unit for measuring mass
liter a unit for measuring how much
       liquid a container will hold
degree a unit of temperature

Dear Family,

During the next few weeks our math class will be learning about measurement.

You can expect to see homework that provides practice with estimating and measuring length, as well as with estimating weight, mass, and capacity. There will also be homework that provides practice with reading a thermometer.

As we learn about measuring length and standard units, you may wish to point out to your child everyday items that are about the same length as the standard units. This will help them remember the various lengths of the units.

Standard Units of Length	Everyday Referents
inch	small paperclip
foot (12 inches)	piece of writing paper
centimeter	pencil eraser
meter (100 centimeters)	giant step

Sincerely,

Name _____

You can use paper clips or crayons to measure the length of a pencil.

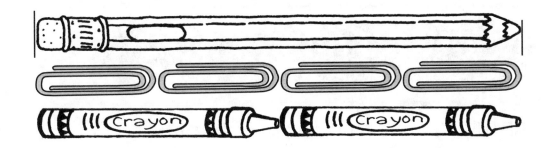

This pencil is about 4 paper clips or about 2 crayons long.

Complete the chart.
Estimate first.
Then measure the object.

		Length in Paper Clips		Length in Crayons	
		Estimate	Measure	Estimate	Measure
1.	paper	about _____	about _____	about _____	about _____
2.	desk top	about _____	about _____	about _____	about _____
3.	math book	about _____	about _____	about _____	about _____
4.	_____	about _____	about _____	about _____	about _____

Estimate the length. Use pennies to measure. Complete.

5.

Estimate about _____ pennies   **Measure** about __7__ pennies

6.

Estimate about _____ pennies   **Measure** about _____ pennies

7.

Estimate about _____ pennies   **Measure** about _____ pennies

| Problem Solving |
| Reasoning |

8. Barb wants to measure the length of her shoe. First she uses crayons to measure. Then she uses pennies. Does Barb use more crayons or more pennies? Explain.

_____

_____

★ Test Prep

Jenny measured the length of her thumb.
Mark a reasonable length.

9

    ○ about 1 penny   ○ about 2 or 3 pennies

    ○ about 10 pennies   ○ about 100 pennies

Name _____

Inch and Foot

This is an inch ruler.
Each number marks
I inch.

←—I inch—→

Write the numbers.

1. This ruler is ☐ 4 ☐ inches long.

Mark the inches.

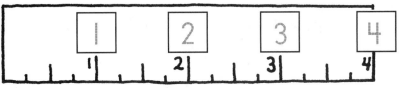

2. This ruler is ☐ inches long.

Mark the inches.

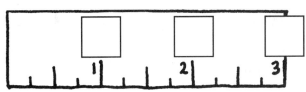

Use a ruler. How long is each rod?

3. about ☐ 5 ☐ inches

4. about ☐ inches

5. about ☐ inches

Use a ruler. How far has each ant gone?

6. about ☐ inches

7. about ☐ inches

Unit 5 • Lesson 2

(one hundred seventeen) **117**

Most inch rulers are **12** inches long.
12 inches = **1** foot

Use a ruler. Measure and record.

8. across your desk

about _____ feet

9. across your teacher's desk

about _____ feet

10. from your desk to the next desk

about _____ feet

11. from the top of a table to the floor

about _____ feet

12. across a window

about _____ feet

13. across a bookshelf

about _____ feet

Problem Solving Reasoning

14. Which is longer, your desk or your teacher's desk?

How do you know? _____

_____

★ Test Prep

About how many inches? Mark the space for your answer.
If the answer is **not here**, mark the space for **NH**.

15

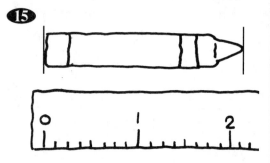

1 ○   2 ○   3 ○   NH ○

Name _____

Problem Solving Plan
1. Understand 2. Decide 3. Solve 4. Look back

Solve. Write + or − in each ◯.

1. There are **15** inches of plaid ribbon. There are **6** inches of lace ribbon. How many more inches of plaid ribbon are there than lace ribbon?

   Think Do you need to add or subtract? _____subtract_____

   15 ⊝ 6 = _____

   Answer _____ more inches

2. Wai's desk measures **2** feet across. Charlton's desk measures **2** feet across. How many feet across are both desks together?

   Think Do you need to add or subtract? _____

   2 ◯ 2 = _____

   Answer _____ feet

3. Colin has **13** inches of ribbon. He uses **7** inches for a bow. How many inches of ribbon does he have left?

   Think Do you need to add or subtract? _____

   13 ◯ 7 = _____

   Answer _____ inches

4. The red ant traveled **17** inches. The black ant traveled **8** inches. How much farther did the red ant go than the black ant?

   Think Do you need to add or subtract? _____

   17 ◯ 8 = _____

   Answer _____ inches farther

Solve.

5. Our computer keyboard is **13** paper clips long. Our math book is **8** paper clips long. How much longer is our keyboard than our math book?

13 ◯ 8 = _____

Answer _____ more paper clips

6. Jesse has **14** inches of string. He uses **5** inches of string to wrap a present. How many inches of string are left?

14 ◯ 5 = _____

Answer _____ inches

7. There are **5** inches of red ribbon. There are **7** inches of white ribbon. There are **5** inches of blue ribbon. How many inches of ribbon are there in all?

5 ◯ 7 ◯ 5 = _____

Answer _____ inches

8. It is **16** feet from the chart to the wall. It is **8** feet from the chart to the door. How many more feet is it from the chart to the wall than to the door?

16 ◯ 8 = _____

Answer _____ more feet

Extend Your Thinking

9. What strategies did you use to solve the problems? _____

_____

_____

_____

Work with a partner.
Fill in the chart.
Estimate first, then measure.
Use a centimeter ruler.

		My Estimate in Centimeters	Measurement in Centimeters
1.	the length of your thumb	about _____	about _____
2.	the length of your pencil	about _____	about _____
3.	the length of your math book	about _____	about _____
4.	the width of your math book	about _____	about _____
5.	the length of your shoe	about _____	about _____
6.			
7.			
8.			

You may want to measure some other objects.
Add them to the chart above.

A ruler 100 centimeters long is a meter stick.

100 centimeters **= 1 meter**

Use a meter stick.
Measure and record.

9. from your desk to the door

about _____ meters

10. from wall to wall

about _____ meters

11. from bottom to top of door

about _____ meters

12. across the chalkboard

about _____ meters

 Quick Check

Measure and record.

1. Use small paper clips.

about ____ paper clips

2. Use an inch ruler.

about ____ inches

3. Use a centimeter ruler.

about ____ centimeters

Problem

How many of the tiles do you need to cover this floor?

1 Understand

I need to find out how many tiles
I need to cover the floor.

2 Decide

I can guess then check.

3 Solve

I'll make a guess.

My guess is _____ tiles.
I'll cut out the tiles and cover the floor.
I'll count the tiles to check how many I used.

I used __15__ tiles to cover the floor.

4 Look back

I know that I needed **15** tiles to cover the floor.
My answer makes sense.

How many tiles do you need?
Guess then check.

1.

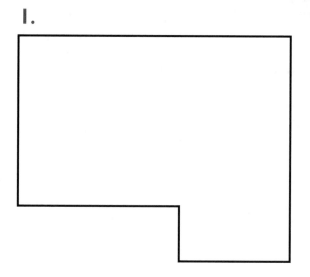

guess _____ check _____

2.

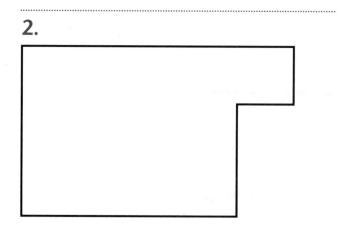

guess _____ check _____

3. Which floor has a larger area, the floor in problem 1 or in

problem 2? Explain. _____

_____

_____

I pound

A  weighs less than a pound.

A 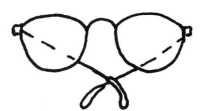 weighs more than a pound.

Ring the best estimate.

1.

(less than a pound)   about a pound   more than a pound

2.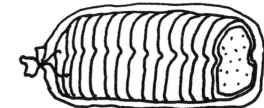

less than a pound   about a pound   more than a pound

3.

less than a pound   about a pound   more than a pound

4.

less than a pound   about a pound   more than a pound

★ Test Prep

Which one weighs more than a pound? Mark the best estimate.

5

◯   ◯   ◯   ◯

Name _____

Kilogram

A **kilogram** is a unit for measuring mass.

less
than a
kilogram

about
a
kilogram

more
than a
kilogram

Ring the best estimate.

1.

(less than a kilogram)

about a kilogram

more than a kilogram

2.

less than a kilogram

about a kilogram

more than a kilogram

3.

less than a kilogram

about a kilogram

more than a kilogram

4.

less than a kilogram

about a kilogram

more than a kilogram

★ Test Prep

Which one has a mass of less than a kilogram? Mark the best estimate.

❺

○

○

○

○

126 (one hundred twenty-six)

Unit 5 • Lesson 7

Name _____

 2 cups = 1 pint

 4 cups = 1 quart

  2 pints = 1 quart

  4 quarts = 1 gallon

Fill in the blank.

1.   4 cups = _2_ pints

2.   1 pint = ____ cups

3.   ____ pints = 1 quart

4.   ____ quarts = 1 gallon

5.   2 quarts = ____ cups

6.   ____ cups = 1 quart

7.   4 pints = ____ quarts

8.   ____ pints = 3 quarts

☑ **Quick Check**

Ring the best estimate.

1.

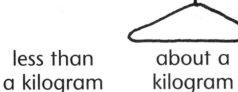

less than   about a   more than
a pound   pound   a pound

2.

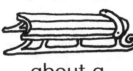

less than   about a   more than
a kilogram   kilogram   a kilogram

Fill in the blank.

3. 8 cups = ____ quarts

Unit 5 • Lesson 8

Name_____

Liter

I liter

A **liter** is a unit for measuring how much liquid a container will hold.

Try this experiment.

Find **5** jars or containers and label them 1–5. Pour water from each one into a liter measure.

Which ones hold more than **I** liter?

Which ones hold less than **I** liter?

Does any jar hold the same as the liter measure?

		Less than I liter	I liter	More than I liter
1.	Jar 1			
2.	Jar 2			
3.	Jar 3			
4.	Jar 4			
5.	Jar 5			

★ Test Prep

How much water does a large fish tank hold?
Mark under your best estimate.

6
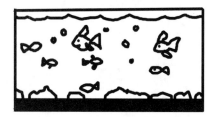

less than
I liter
○

I liter
○

more than
I liter
○

128 (one hundred twenty-eight)

Unit 5 • Lesson 9

Name _____

Temperature

Temperature can be measured in **degrees** Fahrenheit.

Read these Fahrenheit thermometers.

1.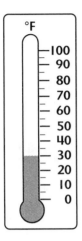

_30_ degrees

2.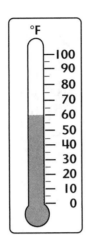

_____ degrees

3.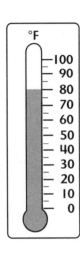

_____ degrees

4.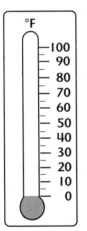

_____ degrees

5.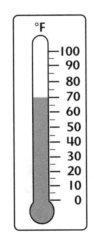

_____ degrees

6.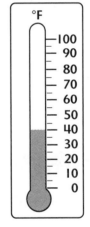

_____ degrees

Measure the temperature.

7. in your classroom _____

8. outside in the morning _____

9. outside at noon _____

Temperature can also be measured in **degrees** Celsius.

Read these Celsius thermometers.

10.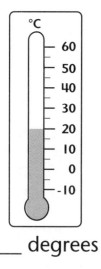

_____ degrees

11.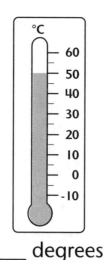

_____ degrees

12.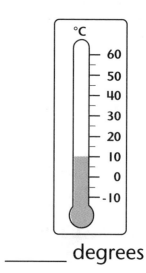

_____ degrees

**Problem Solving
Reasoning**

13. How are Celsius thermometers and Fahrenheit thermometers

alike? _____

_____

★ Test Prep

Read the Fahrenheit thermometer. Mark the correct temperature.

14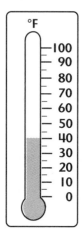

○ 20 degrees   ○ 30 degrees

○ 40 degrees   ○ 50 degrees

Name _____

Measure with a centimeter ruler.

1.

about _____ centimeters

2.

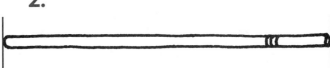

about _____ centimeters

Measure with an inch ruler.

3.

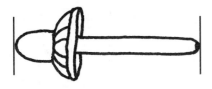

about _____ inches

4.

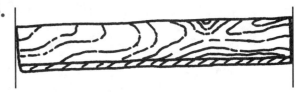

about _____ inches

Ring the best estimate.

5.

| less than a pound | about a pound | more than a pound |

6.

| less than a pound | about a pound | more than a pound |

7.

| less than a kilogram | about a kilogram | more than a kilogram |

8.

| less than a kilogram | about a kilogram | more than a kilogram |

Use an inch ruler. How far has each ladybug gone?

9. about ☐ inches

10. about ☐ inches

Read each Fahrenheit thermometer.

11.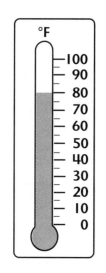

_____ degrees

12.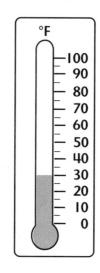

_____ degrees

13.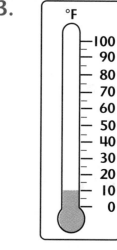

_____ degrees

Problem Solving
Reasoning   Solve. Write + or − in each ◯.

14. There are **6** centimeters of red licorice. There are **5** centimeters of black licorice. How many centimeters of licorice are there in all?

6 ◯ 5 = ____

_____ centimeters

15. Courtney has **12** feet of rope. She uses **6** feet of rope in her science project. How many feet of rope does Courtney have left?

12 ◯ 6 = ____

_____ feet

132 (one hundred thirty-two)

Name _____

Complete.

❶

66	68	80	86
○	○	○	○

---

❷

70¢ > 30¢	41¢ > 14¢	79¢ > 97¢	35¢ < 42¢
○	○	○	○

---

❸

○ 7 dimes and 6 pennies   ○ 7 dimes and 8 pennies

○ 7 dimes and 7 pennies   ○ 7 dimes and 9 pennies

---

❹

17 pieces	16 pieces	19 pieces	18 pieces
○	○	○	○

---

❺

8 more rocks	6 more rocks	9 more rocks	7 more rocks
○	○	○	○

Complete.

6

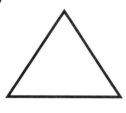

square	triangle	rectangle	circle
○	○	○	○

7

$\dfrac{1}{5}$	$\dfrac{2}{5}$	$\dfrac{3}{5}$	$\dfrac{5}{5}$
○	○	○	○

8

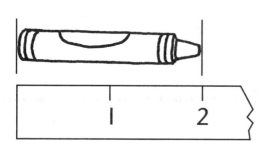

1	2	3	4
○	○	○	○

Decide on an answer. Mark the space for your answer.
If the answer is **not here**, mark the space for **NH**.

9

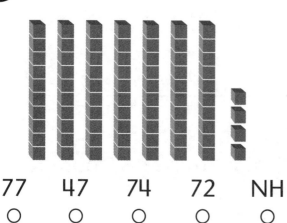

77	47	74	72	NH
○	○	○	○	○

10

$$9 + (4 + 3) = \boxed{}$$

19	16	18	17	NH
○	○	○	○	○

134 (one hundred thirty-four)

Unit 5 • Cumulative Review

UNIT 6 • TABLE OF CONTENTS

2-Digit Addition

We will be using this vocabulary:

regroup group 10 ones into 1 ten

Dear Family,

During the next few weeks our math class will be learning about 2-digit addition with and without regrouping. (Other words for regrouping include carrying and trading.)

You can expect to see homework that provides practice with 2-digit addition. There will also be homework that provides practice with adding money.

As we learn about 2-digit addition, you may wish to keep the following as a guide.

Adding 2-digit Numbers

1. Look at the ones.

2. Can you regroup? If so, regroup.

3. Add the ones, then the tens.

Tens	Ones
1	
5	4
+ 3	8
9	2

Sincerely,

Use what you know to add tens.

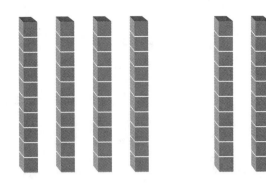

4 tens   +   **2** tens = **6** tens

40   +   **20**   = **60**

How does knowing **4 + 2 = 6** help you add **40 + 20**?

Add.

1. **2** tens + **6** tens = __8__ tens

    20 + **60** = __80__

2. **4** tens + **3** tens = ____ tens

    40 + **30** = ____

3. **5** tens + **4** tens = ____ tens

    50 + **40** = ____

4. **7** tens + **1** ten = ____ tens

    70 + **10** = ____

5. **20 + 30** = ____

    30 + 10 = ____

    20 + 70 = ____

6. **30 + 30** = ____

    60 + 30 = ____

    80 + 10 = ____

Add.

7. $30 + 10 = \underline{40}$

    $30 + 15 = \underline{\hphantom{00}}$

    $30 + 20 = \underline{\hphantom{00}}$

    $30 + 25 = \underline{\hphantom{00}}$

    $30 + 30 = \underline{\hphantom{00}}$

    $30 + 35 = \underline{\hphantom{00}}$

    $30 + 40 = \underline{\hphantom{00}}$

8. $35 + 50 = \underline{\hphantom{00}}$

    $40 + 35 = \underline{\hphantom{00}}$

    $50 + 25 = \underline{\hphantom{00}}$

    $15 + 40 = \underline{\hphantom{00}}$

    $20 + 60 = \underline{\hphantom{00}}$

    $40 + 50 = \underline{\hphantom{00}}$

    $55 + 20 = \underline{\hphantom{00}}$

Problem Solving
Reasoning

9. What pattern to you see in exercise 7? _____

    _____

    _____

    _____

    _____

★ Test Prep

Decide on an answer. Mark the space for your answer.
If the answer is **not here**, mark the space for **NH**.

10.
$40 + 40 = \square$

50	60	80	90	NH
○	○	○	○	○

Unit 6 • Lesson 1

Name _____

Add.

1.

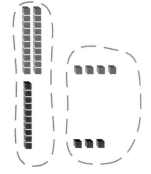

Tens	Ones
2	4
+ 1	3
3	7

2.

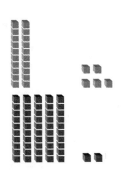

Tens	Ones
2	5
+ 5	2

3.

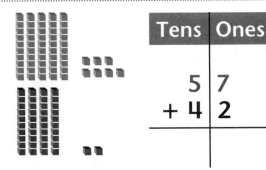

Tens	Ones
6	3
+ 3	4

4.

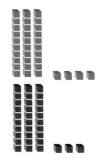

Tens	Ones
3	4
+ 3	3

5.

Tens	Ones
5	7
+ 4	2

6.

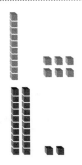

Tens	Ones
1	6
+ 2	2

7.

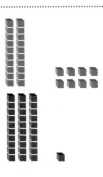

Tens	Ones
2	8
+ 3	1

8.

Tens	Ones
3	2
+ 4	1

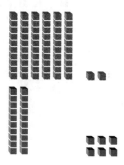

Tens	Ones
6	2
+ 2	6
8	8

```
  62
 +26
 ─────
  88  ←——— sum
```

Add.

9.
```
  13
 +14
 ────
  27
```
```
  26
 +11
 ────
```
```
  35
 +12
 ────
```
```
  65
 +11
 ────
```
```
  54
 +13
 ────
```

10.
```
  11
 +41
 ────
```
```
  22
 +42
 ────
```
```
  42
 +23
 ────
```
```
  52
 +14
 ────
```
```
  30
 +15
 ────
```

11.
```
  40
 +31
 ────
```
```
  52
 +20
 ────
```
```
  10
 +53
 ────
```
```
  34
 +40
 ────
```
```
  10
 +50
 ────
```

12.
```
  12
 +25
 ────
```
```
  26
 +42
 ────
```
```
  75
 +13
 ────
```
```
  23
 +44
 ────
```
```
  26
 +52
 ────
```

13.
```
  23
 +43
 ────
```
```
  36
 +41
 ────
```
```
  35
 +12
 ────
```
```
  52
 +17
 ────
```
```
  60
 +30
 ────
```

Add.

14.
$$41 + 11$$
$$11 + 30$$
$$52 + 44$$
$$64 + 21$$
$$71 + 26$$

15.
$$71 + 24$$
$$44 + 12$$
$$27 + 51$$
$$24 + 43$$
$$22 + 52$$

16.
$$46 + 42$$
$$34 + 21$$
$$18 + 61$$
$$27 + 62$$
$$93 + 6$$

17.
$$35 + 44$$
$$36 + 12$$
$$87 + 2$$
$$30 + 12$$
$$40 + 11$$

18.
$$54 + 31$$
$$65 + 4$$
$$82 + 16$$
$$60 + 10$$
$$70 + 12$$

19.
$$13 + 22$$
$$24 + 30$$
$$12 + 54$$
$$40 + 10$$
$$10 + 11$$

Unit 6 • Lesson 2

20. Tony has **42** markers.
Xiao has **17** markers.
How many markers do
they have in all?

_____ markers

21. Lisa grows **33** tomatoes.
Katarina grows **45** carrots.
How many vegetables do they
grow in all?

_____ vegetables

22. Su Lin collects stamps.
She collects **40** red stamps
and **30** blue stamps.
How many stamps has she
collected?

_____ stamps

23. Kate tosses **2** counters on the
game board to score points.
Her total score is **60** points.
Mark X where her counters
may have landed.

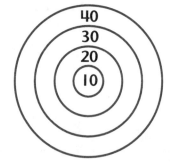

★ Test Prep

Solve. Mark the space for your answer.

24

$$\begin{array}{r} 54 \\ +32 \\ \hline \square \end{array}$$

75   ○   86   ○   22   ○   96   ○

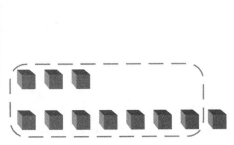

	T	O
	¹4	3
+		8
	5	1

This makes another ten.
So regroup.

Regroup and add.

1.

	T	O
	2	2
+		9
	3	

2.

	T	O
	4	7
+		4

3.

	T	O
	5	5
+		6

4.

	T	O
	7	3
+		9

5.

	T	O
	4	6
+		4

6.

	T	O
	8	4
+		8

7.

	T	O
	3	4
+		6

8.

	T	O
	7	8
+		3

9.

	T	O
	3	9
+		2

How can you use mental math to find the sums?
Try counting on.

10.
$$87 + 3 = 90$$

$$18 + 3$$

$$39 + 2$$

$$29 + 3$$

$$47 + 3$$

11.
$$28 + 3$$

$$29 + 1$$

$$59 + 3$$

$$88 + 2$$

$$69 + 1$$

☑ Quick Check

Add.

1.
$$50 + 35$$

2.
$$41 + 7$$

3.
$$47 + 22$$

4.
$$53 + 8$$

Name _____

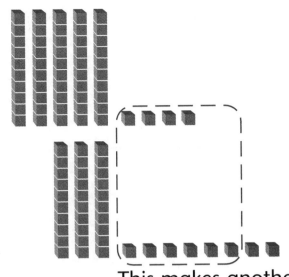

This makes another ten. So regroup.

	T	O
1		
	5	4
+	3	8
	9	2

Add. Start with the ones.

1.

	T	O
1		
	5	6
+	2	5
	8	1

2.

	T	O
	2	4
+	5	7

3.

	T	O
	6	7
+	2	3

4.

	T	O
	6	7
+	2	4

5.

	T	O
	2	9
+	1	2

6.

	T	O
	4	6
+	1	6

7.

	T	O
	3	8
+	2	3

8.

	T	O
	5	6
+	1	6

9.

	T	O
	3	1
+	1	9

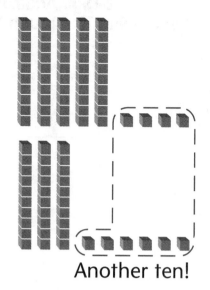

Tens	Ones
5	4
+ 3	6
9	0

$$\begin{array}{r} 54 \\ + 36 \\ \hline 90 \end{array}$$

Another ten!

Find the sum.

10.
$$\begin{array}{r} 68 \\ +14 \\ \hline 82 \end{array}$$

11.
$$\begin{array}{r} 39 \\ +23 \\ \hline \end{array}$$

12.
$$\begin{array}{r} 48 \\ +14 \\ \hline \end{array}$$

13.
$$\begin{array}{r} 44 \\ +26 \\ \hline \end{array}$$

14.
$$\begin{array}{r} 53 \\ +19 \\ \hline \end{array}$$

15.
$$\begin{array}{r} 22 \\ +29 \\ \hline \end{array}$$

16.
$$\begin{array}{r} 44 \\ +28 \\ \hline \end{array}$$

17.
$$\begin{array}{r} 37 \\ +44 \\ \hline \end{array}$$

18.
$$\begin{array}{r} 64 \\ +28 \\ \hline \end{array}$$

19.
$$\begin{array}{r} 17 \\ +33 \\ \hline \end{array}$$

20.
$$\begin{array}{r} 43 \\ +19 \\ \hline \end{array}$$

21.
$$\begin{array}{r} 23 \\ +28 \\ \hline \end{array}$$

22.
$$\begin{array}{r} 45 \\ +27 \\ \hline \end{array}$$

23.
$$\begin{array}{r} 29 \\ +32 \\ \hline \end{array}$$

24.
$$\begin{array}{r} 56 \\ +26 \\ \hline \end{array}$$

25.
$$\begin{array}{r} 67 \\ +24 \\ \hline \end{array}$$

★ Test Prep

Solve. Mark the space for your answer.

 26

$$\begin{array}{r} 43 \\ +27 \\ \hline \square \end{array}$$

60 ○   69 ○   70 ○   80 ○

146 (one hundred forty-six)

Name _____

Adding a 1-Digit Number with Regrouping

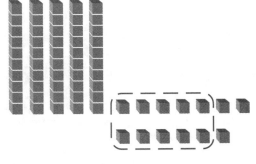

Another ten!

	T	O
	¹5	7
+		6
	6	3

Regroup and add.

1.
	T	O
	4	8
+		6
	5	4

2.
	T	O
	6	9
+		4

3.
	T	O
	2	7
+		7

4.
	T	O
	3	7
+		7

5.
	T	O
	4	4
+		9

6.
	T	O
	7	8
+		5

7.
	T	O
	2	5
+		8

8.
	T	O
	1	8
+		6

9.
	T	O
	5	6
+		7

Unit 6 • Lesson 5

(one hundred forty-seven) 147

Add.

	T	O

10.
	6	8
+		6
	7	4

68
+ 6
74

74
+ 8

57
+ 7

35
+ 7

42
+ 9

11. 85
+ 8

47
+ 7

16
+ 7

36
+ 8

57
+ 5

69
+ 5

12. 65
+ 9

39
+ 2

79
+ 5

54
+ 7

17
+ 7

49
+ 5

Problem Solving Reasoning Use mental math. Count on 1, 2, or 3 to find the sum.

13. 37
+ 3

79
+ 2

28
+ 3

38
+ 3

59
+ 1

77
+ 3

★ **Test Prep**

Solve. Mark the space for your answer.

14

25
+ 9
☐

24
○

34
○

35
○

38
○

Name _____

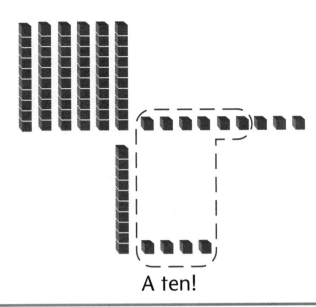

A ten!

	T	O
	¹	
	6	9
+	1	4
	8	3

Add. Start with the ones.

1.

T	O
¹	
4	9
+ 3	5
8	4

2.

T	O
5	8
+ 1	5

3.

T	O
2	5
+ 3	8

4.

T	O
1	9
+ 1	4

5.

T	O
3	5
+ 2	9

6.

T	O
3	6
+ 2	7

7.

T	O
2	5
+ 3	9

8.

T	O
3	6
+ 1	8

9.

T	O
1	9
+ 4	5

Add.

10.

T	O
3	7
+ 2	7
6	4

26
+38

46
+17

79
+15

34
+29

11.   39
+25

67
+27

28
+15

46
+28

57
+27

12.   35
+29

46
+27

17
+27

34
+39

58
+25

Problem Solving
Reasoning Solve.

13. There are **28** basketballs in the locker room.
There are **35** basketballs in the gymnasium.
How many basketballs are there in all?   _____ basketballs

 Quick Check

Add.

1.   57
+24

2.   78
+ 6

3.   18
+45

4.   29
+25

Name _____

	T	O
	1	
	2	9
+		6
	3	5

	T	O
	1	
	3	8
+		8
	4	6

Add.

T	O

1.

	T	O
	1	
	2	7
+		9
		6

$$\begin{array}{r} 79 \\ + \ 6 \\ \hline \end{array}$$

$$\begin{array}{r} 58 \\ + \ 8 \\ \hline \end{array}$$

$$\begin{array}{r} 16 \\ + \ 9 \\ \hline \end{array}$$

$$\begin{array}{r} 89 \\ + \ 7 \\ \hline \end{array}$$

2.

$$\begin{array}{r} 37 \\ + \ 8 \\ \hline \end{array}$$

$$\begin{array}{r} 27 \\ + \ 9 \\ \hline \end{array}$$

$$\begin{array}{r} 26 \\ + \ 9 \\ \hline \end{array}$$

$$\begin{array}{r} 69 \\ + \ 6 \\ \hline \end{array}$$

$$\begin{array}{r} 88 \\ + \ 7 \\ \hline \end{array}$$

3.

$$\begin{array}{r} 68 \\ + \ 8 \\ \hline \end{array}$$

$$\begin{array}{r} 29 \\ + \ 4 \\ \hline \end{array}$$

$$\begin{array}{r} 17 \\ + \ 9 \\ \hline \end{array}$$

$$\begin{array}{r} 67 \\ + \ 8 \\ \hline \end{array}$$

$$\begin{array}{r} 56 \\ + \ 9 \\ \hline \end{array}$$

4.

$$\begin{array}{r} 28 \\ + \ 7 \\ \hline \end{array}$$

$$\begin{array}{r} 37 \\ + \ 9 \\ \hline \end{array}$$

$$\begin{array}{r} 47 \\ + \ 9 \\ \hline \end{array}$$

$$\begin{array}{r} 19 \\ + \ 6 \\ \hline \end{array}$$

$$\begin{array}{r} 38 \\ + \ 7 \\ \hline \end{array}$$

5.

$$\begin{array}{r} 59 \\ + \ 7 \\ \hline \end{array}$$

$$\begin{array}{r} 19 \\ + \ 6 \\ \hline \end{array}$$

$$\begin{array}{r} 28 \\ + \ 7 \\ \hline \end{array}$$

$$\begin{array}{r} 47 \\ + \ 8 \\ \hline \end{array}$$

$$\begin{array}{r} 67 \\ + \ 9 \\ \hline \end{array}$$

Unit 6 • Lesson 7

Add.

6.
$$36 + 19 = 55$$

$$57 + 19$$

$$38 + 17$$

$$29 + 46$$

$$38 + 17$$

7.
$$19 + 67$$

$$47 + 18$$

$$58 + 18$$

$$76 + 19$$

$$37 + 19$$

8.
$$76 + 19$$

$$17 + 49$$

$$68 + 17$$

$$19 + 47$$

$$79 + 17$$

9.
$$29 + 16$$

$$38 + 48$$

$$47 + 29$$

$$58 + 38$$

$$67 + 18$$

Problem Solving Reasoning Solve.

10. Kevin picks **36** apples. Dee picks **39** apples. How many apples do they pick in all?

_____

11. The red team counts **28** caterpillars. The blue team counts **38** caterpillars. How many caterpillars are there in all?

_____

★ Test Prep

Solve. Mark the space under your answer.

12.

$$48 + 18 = \boxed{}$$

56	66	68	78
○	○	○	○

	T	O
	¹4	8
+		9
	5	7

	T	O
	¹3	9
+		9
	4	8

Add.

	T	O

1.
$$\begin{array}{r} 39 \\ +\ 8 \\ \hline 47 \end{array}$$
$$\begin{array}{r} 69 \\ +\ 9 \\ \hline \end{array}$$
$$\begin{array}{r} 59 \\ +\ 8 \\ \hline \end{array}$$
$$\begin{array}{r} 88 \\ +\ 9 \\ \hline \end{array}$$
$$\begin{array}{r} 49 \\ +\ 9 \\ \hline \end{array}$$

2.
$$\begin{array}{r} 39 \\ +\ 9 \\ \hline \end{array}$$
$$\begin{array}{r} 68 \\ +\ 9 \\ \hline \end{array}$$
$$\begin{array}{r} 58 \\ +\ 9 \\ \hline \end{array}$$
$$\begin{array}{r} 29 \\ +\ 8 \\ \hline \end{array}$$
$$\begin{array}{r} 78 \\ +\ 9 \\ \hline \end{array}$$

3.
$$\begin{array}{r} 89 \\ +\ 8 \\ \hline \end{array}$$
$$\begin{array}{r} 49 \\ +\ 8 \\ \hline \end{array}$$
$$\begin{array}{r} 79 \\ +\ 9 \\ \hline \end{array}$$
$$\begin{array}{r} 19 \\ +\ 8 \\ \hline \end{array}$$
$$\begin{array}{r} 59 \\ +\ 9 \\ \hline \end{array}$$

4.
$$\begin{array}{r} 38 \\ +\ 9 \\ \hline \end{array}$$
$$\begin{array}{r} 89 \\ +\ 9 \\ \hline \end{array}$$
$$\begin{array}{r} 18 \\ +\ 9 \\ \hline \end{array}$$
$$\begin{array}{r} 69 \\ +\ 8 \\ \hline \end{array}$$
$$\begin{array}{r} 29 \\ +\ 9 \\ \hline \end{array}$$

Complete.

5. $8 + \underline{\hspace{1cm}} = 17$ $\qquad$ $18 - \underline{\hspace{1cm}} = 9$ $\qquad$ $9 + \underline{\hspace{1cm}} = 17$

6. $9 + \underline{\hspace{1cm}} = 18$ $\qquad$ $17 - \underline{\hspace{1cm}} = 9$ $\qquad$ $17 - \underline{\hspace{1cm}} = 8$

Add.

7.　49　　　　58　　　　68　　　　69　　　　58
　　+28　　　 +19　　　 +29　　　 +19　　　 +39
　　77

8.　39　　　　19　　　　29　　　　49　　　　69
　　+18　　　 +28　　　 +48　　　 +38　　　 +29

9.　39　　　　19　　　　19　　　　78　　　　38
　　+29　　　 +29　　　 +19　　　 +19　　　 +29

| Problem Solving Reasoning | **Solve.** |

10. There are **19** girls at the picnic. There are **18** boys at the picnic. How many children are at the picnic in all?

_____

11. Cathy has **29** pins in her collection. Charlie has **29** pins in his collection, too. How many pins do they have in all?

_____

★ Test Prep

Solve. Mark the space under your answer.

　　29
　 +19
　 [   ]

48　　　　28　　　　38　　　　49
○　　　　 ○　　　　 ○　　　　 ○

Unit 6 • Lesson 8

Name _____   **Adding Money**

Add. Use ¢.

1.
```
  23¢        39¢        55¢        67¢        49¢
+ 38¢      + 18¢      + 25¢      + 27¢      + 32¢
─────      ─────      ─────      ─────      ─────
  61¢
```

2.
```
  47¢        53¢        66¢        29¢        68¢
+ 29¢      + 19¢      + 27¢      + 67¢      + 22¢
─────      ─────      ─────      ─────      ─────
```

How much for both?

3.
```
  39¢
+ 59¢
─────
  98¢
```

4.
```
+ ____
```

5.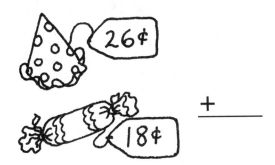
```
+ ____
```

6.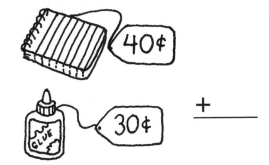
```
+ ____
```

7.
```
+ ____
```

8.
```
+ ____
```

Unit 6 • Lesson 9   (one hundred fifty-five) 155

Find the sum.

9.
$$\begin{array}{r} 27¢ \\ + 18¢ \\ \hline \end{array}$$
$$\begin{array}{r} 39¢ \\ + 46¢ \\ \hline \end{array}$$
$$\begin{array}{r} 71¢ \\ + 19¢ \\ \hline \end{array}$$
$$\begin{array}{r} 26¢ \\ + 35¢ \\ \hline \end{array}$$

10.
$$\begin{array}{r} 73¢ \\ + 17¢ \\ \hline \end{array}$$
$$\begin{array}{r} 92¢ \\ + 7¢ \\ \hline \end{array}$$
$$\begin{array}{r} 66¢ \\ + 26¢ \\ \hline \end{array}$$
$$\begin{array}{r} 29¢ \\ + 69¢ \\ \hline \end{array}$$

Problem Solving Reasoning Solve.

11. Theo spends **63¢** for the ball.
He spends **29¢** for the balloon.
How much does Theo spend for both?

_____

 Quick Check

Solve.

1.
$$\begin{array}{r} 57 \\ + 8 \\ \hline \end{array}$$

2.
$$\begin{array}{r} 53 \\ + 8 \\ \hline \end{array}$$

3.
$$\begin{array}{r} 64 \\ + 19 \\ \hline \end{array}$$

4.
$$\begin{array}{r} 66¢ \\ + 13¢ \\ \hline \end{array}$$

Name _____

Three Addends

Add.

1.

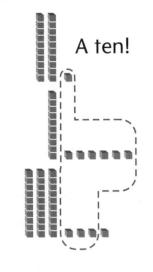

A ten!

T	O
2	1
1	6
+ 3	4
7	

2.

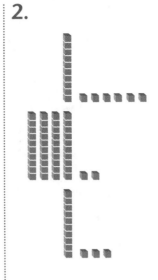

T	O
1	6
4	2
+ 1	3

3.
```
    32        43        41        62
    14        14        25        12
  + 35      + 25      + 26      + 18
```

4.
```
    21        52        64        34
    45        10        12        31
  + 16      + 18      + 16      + 25
```

5.
```
    43        36        43        34
    12        10        20        42
  + 17      + 46      + 18      + 16
```

6.
```
    12        14        37        50
    35        13        11        14
  + 23      + 45      + 24      + 17
```

Add each column. Start with the ones.

7.
T	O
3	2
1	5
+ 2	6
7	3

8.
T	O
2	6
5	3
+ 1	3

9.
T	O
4	4
1	5
+ 3	4

Add.

10.
42	34	51	22	53
33	44	15	13	14
+ 18	+ 12	+ 23	+ 48	+ 23

11.
63	12	42	11	27
13	14	22	51	11
+ 16	+ 27	+ 28	+ 28	+ 53

Problem Solving Reasoning Write an addition story using three addends.

12._____

_____

★ Test Prep

Solve. Mark the space under your answer.
If the answer is **not here**, mark the space for **NH**.

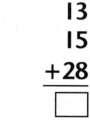

| 13 |
| 15 |
| +28 |
| ☐ |

46   54   56   66   NH

○   ○   ○   ○   ○

Name _____

Problem

Which two jars have
a total of **60** beans?

❶ Understand

I need to find out which two jars have a total of **60** beans.

❷ Decide

I can guess then check.

❸ Solve

First guess: I'll guess Jar A and Jar B. I'll add to check.

$$\begin{array}{r} 25 \\ + 30 \\ \hline 55 \end{array}$$ beans. Too low. I'll guess again.

Second guess: I'll guess Jar B and Jar C. I'll add to check.

$$\begin{array}{r} 30 \\ + 35 \\ \hline 65 \end{array}$$ beans. Too high. I'll guess again.

Third guess: I'll guess Jar A and Jar C. I'll add to check.

$$\begin{array}{r} 25 \\ + 35 \\ \hline 60 \end{array}$$ beans. The guess checks!

Answer Jar __A__ and Jar __C__

❹ Look back

Does my answer make sense? Why?

Solve using guess and check. Show your work.

1. Which two jars have a total of **42** beans?

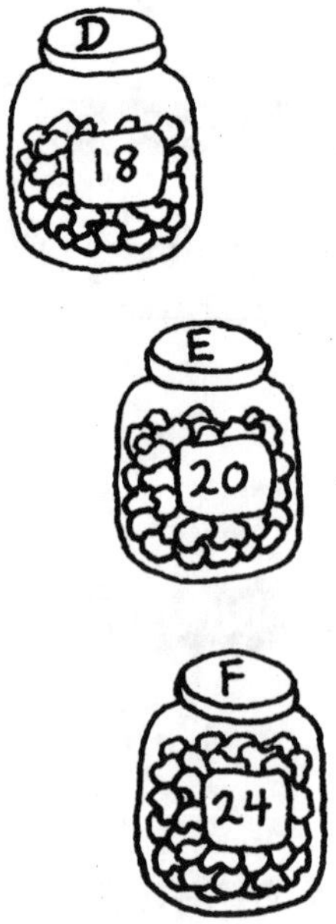

Jar D: 18
Jar E: 20
Jar F: 24

Answer Jar _____ and Jar _____

---

2. Which three jars have a total of **73** beans?

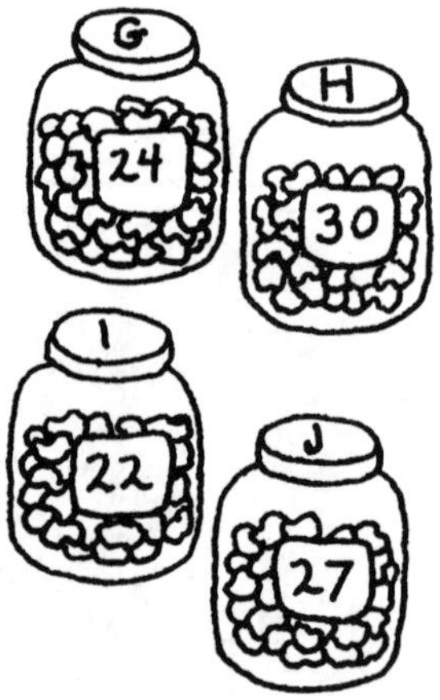

Jar G: 24
Jar H: 30
Jar I: 22
Jar J: 27

Answer Jar _____ and Jar _____ and Jar _____

Problem Solving Plan			
1. Understand	2. Decide	3. Solve	4. Look back

Is there enough information? Ring the answer.
Solve the problems that have enough information.

1. There are **17** red apple trees. There are more yellow apple trees than red apple trees. How many apple trees in all?

   Think Is there enough information?

   enough   (not enough)

   _____ apple trees

2. Ashley sees **35** orange butterflies. Andrew sees **29** yellow butterflies. How many butterflies do they see in all?

   Think Is there enough information?

   (enough)   not enough

   _64_ butterflies

3. There are **12** big carrots. There are **9** little carrots. How many fewer little carrots?

   Think Is there enough information?

   enough   not enough

   _____ fewer little carrots

4. There are **28** white bears. There are **42** brown bears. How many black bears are there?

   Think Is there enough information?

   enough   not enough

   ○
   ___

   _____ black bears

Is there enough information? Ring the answer.
Solve the problems that have enough information.

5. Ling saw **24** elephants. She saw **14** bears. She saw **24** rabbits. How many animals did she see in all?

enough   not enough

◯ ___

_____ animals

6. There are **16** birds in the first tree. There are **27** birds in the second tree. How many birds are in the third tree?

enough   not enough

◯ ___

_____ birds

7. There are **36** red peanuts. There are **5** brown peanuts. How many peanuts in all?

enough   not enough

◯ ___

_____ peanuts

8. There are **11** blue fish in the pond. There are fewer red fish in the pond. How many red fish are there?

enough   not enough

◯ ___

_____ red fish

Extend Your Thinking

9. Choose a problem that does not have enough information. Rewrite it so that it has enough information. Solve.

Name _____

Add.

1. **4** tens + **2** tens = _____ tens

   40 + **20** = _____

2. **3** tens + **5** tens = _____ tens

   30 + **50** = _____

3. **15** + **45** = _____

4. **40** + **35** = _____

Add.

5. $\begin{array}{r} 55 \\ + 13 \\ \hline \end{array}$

6. $\begin{array}{r} 36¢ \\ + 24¢ \\ \hline \end{array}$

7. $\begin{array}{r} 79 \\ + 19 \\ \hline \end{array}$

8. $\begin{array}{r} 47¢ \\ + 19¢ \\ \hline \end{array}$

9. $\begin{array}{r} 38 \\ + 29 \\ \hline \end{array}$

10. $\begin{array}{r} 45 \\ + 27 \\ \hline \end{array}$

11. $\begin{array}{r} 14 \\ + 29 \\ \hline \end{array}$

12. $\begin{array}{r} 15 \\ + 39 \\ \hline \end{array}$

13. $\begin{array}{r} 56 \\ + 19 \\ \hline \end{array}$

14. $\begin{array}{r} 45 \\ + 13 \\ \hline \end{array}$

15. $\begin{array}{r} 46 \\ 22 \\ + 12 \\ \hline \end{array}$

16. $\begin{array}{r} 16¢ \\ 23¢ \\ + 18¢ \\ \hline \end{array}$

17. $\begin{array}{r} 52 \\ 23 \\ + 19 \\ \hline \end{array}$

18. $\begin{array}{r} 42 \\ 34 \\ + 17 \\ \hline \end{array}$

19. $\begin{array}{r} 56 \\ 22 \\ + 19 \\ \hline \end{array}$

Problem Solving Reasoning

Is there enough information? Ring the answer. Solve the problems that have enough information.

20. There are **44** red apples. There are **29** green apples. How many apples are there?

    enough   not enough

    _____ apples

21. There are **37** pears. There are **16** bananas. How many lemons are there?

    enough   not enough

    _____ lemons

Name _____

1

79		81

78   80   82   83
○   ○   ○   ○

2

30	35	40		50	55

39   41   45   60
○   ○   ○   ○

3

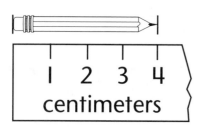

1   2   3   4
centimeters

5   3   4   2
○   ○   ○   ○

Decide on an answer. Mark the space for your answer.
If the answer is **not here**, mark the space for **NH**.

4

$40 + 30 = \square$

60   65   70   75   NH
○   ○   ○   ○   ○

5

$26 + 48 = \square$

63   74   64   73   NH
○   ○   ○   ○   ○

6

$13 + 25 + 46 = \square$

85   74   75   80   NH
○   ○   ○   ○   ○

7

```
X X X
X X X    2/3 of 9 = □
X X X
```

2   3   6   9   NH
○   ○   ○   ○   ○

8

```
X X X X
X X X X    1/3 of 12 = □
X X X X
```

3   4   6   12   NH
○   ○   ○   ○   ○

UNIT 7 • TABLE OF CONTENTS

2-Digit Subtraction

Dear Family,

During the next few weeks our math class will be learning about 2-digit subtraction with and without regrouping.

You can expect to see homework that provides practice with 2-digit subtraction. There will also be homework that provides practice with using money.

As we learn about 2-digit subtraction, you may wish to keep the following as a guide.

To subtract
$$\begin{array}{r} 62 \\ -\ 5 \\ \end{array}$$

1. Regroup a ten.

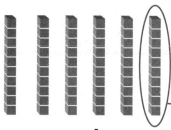

Take apart **1** ten to make **10** ones. **5** tens are left.

$10 + 2 = 12$ ones

2. Subtract.

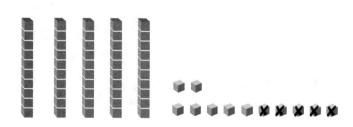

T	O
$\overset{5}{6}$	$\overset{12}{2}$
−	5
5	7

Sincerely,

Use what you know to subtract tens.

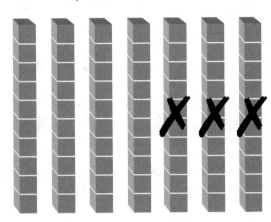

7 tens − **3** tens = **4** tens

70 − 30 = 40

How does knowing **7 − 3 = 4** help you subtract **70 − 30**?

Subtract.

1. **8** tens − **2** tens = ___6___ tens

   80 − 20 = __60__

2. **9** tens − **4** tens = _____ tens

   90 − 40 = ____

3. **7** tens − **5** tens = _____ tens

   70 − 50 = ____

4. **5** tens − **1** ten = _____ tens

   50 − 10 = ____

5. **50 − 30 = ____**

6. **80 − 40 = ____**

7. **90 − 20 = ____**

8. **70 − 40 = ____**

9. **60 − 40 = ____**

10. **90 − 30 = ____**

Subtract.

11. $55 - 10 = \underline{45}$

    $55 - 15 = \underline{\hspace{1cm}}$

    $55 - 20 = \underline{\hspace{1cm}}$

    $55 - 25 = \underline{\hspace{1cm}}$

    $55 - 30 = \underline{\hspace{1cm}}$

    $55 - 35 = \underline{\hspace{1cm}}$

    $55 - 40 = \underline{\hspace{1cm}}$

12. $65 - 20 = \underline{\hspace{1cm}}$

    $75 - 25 = \underline{\hspace{1cm}}$

    $45 - 15 = \underline{\hspace{1cm}}$

    $30 - 20 = \underline{\hspace{1cm}}$

    $55 - 45 = \underline{\hspace{1cm}}$

    $85 - 20 = \underline{\hspace{1cm}}$

    $95 - 30 = \underline{\hspace{1cm}}$

Problem Solving
Reasoning

13. What pattern do you see in exercise 11? _____

_____

_____

_____

★ Test Prep

Decide on an answer. Mark the space for your answer.
If the answer is **not here**, mark the space for **NH**.

14

$90 - 50 = \square$

30	40	50	45	NH
○	○	○	○	○

168 (one hundred sixty-eight)

Unit 7 • Lesson 1

Name _____

Subtract.

1.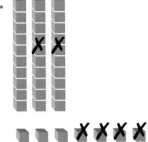

Tens	Ones
3	7
− 2	4
1	3

2.

Tens	Ones
4	5
− 3	1

3.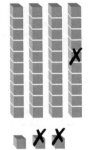

Tens	Ones
4	3
− 1	2

4.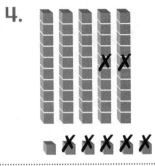

Tens	Ones
5	6
− 2	5

5.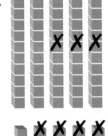

Tens	Ones
5	5
− 3	4

6.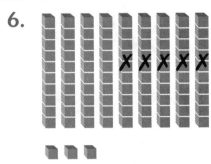

Tens	Ones
9	3
− 5	0

7.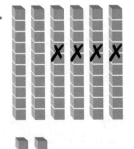

Tens	Ones
6	2
− 4	0

8.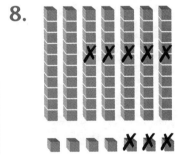

Tens	Ones
7	7
− 5	3

9.

Tens	Ones
8	3
− 2	2

10.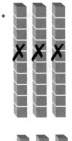

Tens	Ones
3	9
− 3	4

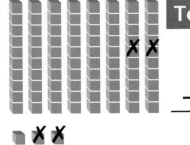

Unit 7 • Lesson 2

(one hundred sixty-nine) 169

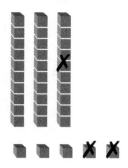

T	O
3	5
−1	2
2	3

$$\begin{array}{r} 3\ 5 \\ -1\ 2 \\ \hline 2\ 3 \end{array}$$ ←difference

---

Subtract.

11.

T	O
2	7
−1	3

T	O
3	6
−1	2

T	O
4	5
−2	4

T	O
6	6
−1	5

T	O
7	7
−3	4

12.

$$\begin{array}{r} 55 \\ -23 \\ \hline \end{array}$$
$$\begin{array}{r} 60 \\ -40 \\ \hline \end{array}$$
$$\begin{array}{r} 49 \\ -28 \\ \hline \end{array}$$
$$\begin{array}{r} 20 \\ -10 \\ \hline \end{array}$$
$$\begin{array}{r} 37 \\ -16 \\ \hline \end{array}$$

13.

$$\begin{array}{r} 98 \\ -34 \\ \hline \end{array}$$
$$\begin{array}{r} 87 \\ -51 \\ \hline \end{array}$$
$$\begin{array}{r} 76 \\ -42 \\ \hline \end{array}$$
$$\begin{array}{r} 64 \\ -31 \\ \hline \end{array}$$
$$\begin{array}{r} 59 \\ -26 \\ \hline \end{array}$$

★ Test Prep

Solve. Decide on an answer. Mark the space for your answer.
If the answer is **not here**, mark the space for **NH**.

$$\begin{array}{r} 78 \\ -26 \\ \hline \boxed{} \end{array}$$

42	43	52	53	NH
○	○	○	○	○

Name _____

Regroup a ten.

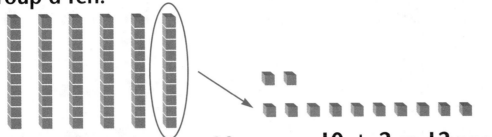

Take apart **1** ten to make **10**
ones. **5** tens are left.

$10 + 2 = 12$ ones

T	O
$\overset{5}{\cancel{6}}$	$\overset{12}{\cancel{2}}$
−	5
5	7

Subtract.

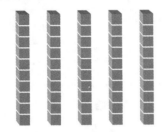

Subtract. Start with the ones.

1.

T	O
$\overset{5}{\cancel{6}}$	$\overset{11}{\cancel{1}}$
−	4
5	7

T	O
2	2
−	7

T	O
6	1
−	9

T	O
8	2
−	3

2.

T	O
8	2
−	8

T	O
7	1
−	7

T	O
2	1
−	8

T	O
5	2
−	5

3.

T	O
4	2
−	3

T	O
2	1
−	7

T	O
7	2
−	9

T	O
9	1
−	8

Find the differences.

4.

T	O
²3̷	¹1̸
−	9
2	2

T	O
4	2
−	8

T	O
6	1
−	6

T	O
4	2
−	7

T	O
5	2
−	6

5.

```
  ⁷8̷¹2
-   7
  7 5
```

```
  3 1
-   9
```

```
  4 1
-   2
```

```
  2 1
-   5
```

```
  6 1
-   3
```

Problem Solving Reasoning

Use mental math. Count back 1, 2, or 3 to find the differences.

6.

```
  5 1
-   2
  4 9
```

```
  4 2
-   3
```

```
  6 1
-   1
```

```
  2 2
-   1
```

```
  8 1
-   3
```

☑ **Quick Check**

Subtract.

1.
```
  9 4
- 6 0
```

2.
```
  8 9
-   6
```

3.
```
  7 4
- 5 4
```

4.
```
  6 2
-   7
```

Name _____

Regroup a ten.

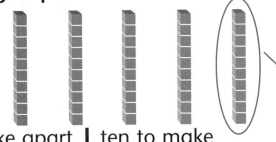

Take apart **1** ten to make
10 ones. **4** tens are left.

$10 + 2 = 12$ ones

```
   T | O
   4 | 12
   5̶ | 2̶
 - 2 | 7
 ------
   2 | 5
```

Subtract.

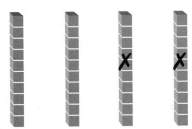

Subtract. Start with the ones.

1.

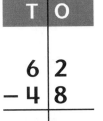

```
   T | O
   4 | 12
   5 | 2
 - 1 | 7
 ------
   3 | 5
```

```
 T | O
 7 | 2
-4 | 5
```

```
 T | O
 8 | 1
-5 | 2
```

```
 T | O
 4 | 2
-1 | 9
```

2.

```
 T | O
 6 | 2
-4 | 8
```

```
 T | O
 7 | 2
-4 | 4
```

```
 T | O
 6 | 2
-4 | 3
```

```
 T | O
 8 | 1
-5 | 6
```

3.

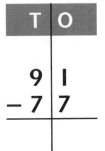

```
 T | O
 9 | 1
-7 | 7
```

```
 T | O
 7 | 2
-5 | 8
```

```
 T | O
 7 | 2
-5 | 9
```

```
 T | O
 9 | 1
-2 | 4
```

Unit 7 • Lesson 4

(one hundred seventy-three) 173

Find each difference.

4.

T	O
²3̸	¹²2̸
– 1	3
	1̶9̶

T	O
6	1
– 3	3

T	O
8	1
– 2	8

T	O
9	2
– 7	6

5.

²3̸ ¹²2̸
– 1 9
1̶3̶

92
– 73

42
– 15

91
– 29

62
– 26

6.

72
– 48

81
– 26

92
– 64

91
– 33

51
– 18

Problem Solving Reasoning | Solve. Use any strategy.

7. Jeffrey has **71** stamps in his collection. He sends **15** stamps to his pen pal in China. How many stamps does Jeffrey have left?

_____ stamps

8. Carmelita has **42** bowls in her pottery collection. She gives **19** bowls to her friend. How many bowls does Carmelita have left?

_____ bowls

★ Test Prep

Solve. Decide on an answer. Mark the space for your answer.
If the answer is **not here**, mark the space for **NH**.

 9

82
– 46
☐

26   36   46   56   NH
○   ○   ○   ○   ○

Unit 7 • Lesson 4

Name _____

Regroup a ten.

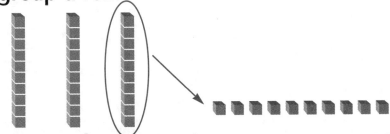

Take apart **1** ten to make
10 ones. **2** tens are left.

$$10 + 0 = 10 \text{ ones}$$

```
        T | O           T | O
        2  10           2  10
        3  0            3  0
      - 1  3          - 1  3
      ---------       ---------
        1  7            1 7
```

Subtract.

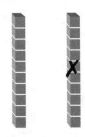

Subtract. Start with the ones.

1.
```
  T | O        T | O        T | O        T | O        T | O
  3   10
  4   0          5  0         6  1         8  0         3  1
- 2   6        -    7       - 3  3       - 6  7       - 1  6
---------      --------     --------     --------     --------
```

2.
```
   52          40           30           92           80
 - 33        - 29         - 17         - 66         -  8
```

3.
```
   60          50           42           30           90
 - 27        - 38         - 15         - 18         -  7
```

4.
```
   80          90           70           60           42
 - 55        - 67         -  4         -  9         - 17
```

Now try these.

5.
$$71 - 43$$ $$92 - 64$$ $$60 - 8$$ $$90 - 63$$ $$62 - 25$$ $$80 - 7$$

6.
$$51 - 29$$ $$50 - 17$$ $$96 - 81$$ $$70 - 45$$ $$80 - 8$$ $$81 - 52$$

7.
$$62 - 48$$ $$87 - 16$$ $$70 - 4$$ $$60 - 3$$ $$98 - 73$$ $$81 - 56$$

Problem Solving Reasoning Solve. Use any strategy.

8. There are **40** children on the school bus. At the first stop, **7** children get off. How many children are left on the bus?

_____ children

9. There are **70** children at the picnic. After lunch, **22** children play kickball. How many children do not play kickball?

_____ children

★ Test Prep

Solve. Decide on an answer. Mark the space for your answer. If the answer is **not here**, mark the space for **NH**.

10
$$90 - 24 \boxed{}$$

56 ○   64 ○   66 ○   76 ○   NH ○

176 (one hundred seventy-six)

Unit 7 • Lesson 5

Name _____

Solve.

1. Had: **50¢**

   Bought: **25¢** 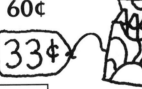 PAPER

   Had: [25] ¢ left

2. Had: **62¢**

   Bought: **35¢**  PARTY

   Had: [ ] ¢ left

3. Had: **21¢**

   Bought: **17¢**

   Had: [ ] ¢ left

4. Had: **52¢**

   Bought: **12¢**

   Had: [ ] ¢ left

5. Had: **60¢**

   Bought: **33¢**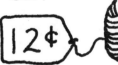

   Had: [ ] ¢ left

6. Had: **72¢**

   Bought: **59¢**

   Had: [ ] ¢ left

7. Had: **32¢**

   Bought: **21¢**

   Had: [ ] ¢ left

8. Had: **41¢**

   Bought: **31¢**

   Had: [ ] ¢ left

Solve.

9. How much less does 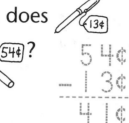 cost than ?

$$\begin{array}{r} 5\ 4\cancel{c} \\ -\ 1\ 3\cancel{c} \\ \hline 4\ 1\cancel{c} \end{array}$$

10. How much more does cost than ?

11. How much more does cost than ?

12. How much less for than for ?

Solve. Use any strategy you choose.

13. The pin costs **71¢**. The sticker costs **59¢**. How much more does

the pin cost than the sticker? _____ ¢ more

 Quick Check

Subtract.

1.
$$\begin{array}{r} 8\ 1 \\ -\ 6\ 7 \\ \hline \end{array}$$

2.
$$\begin{array}{r} 7\ 0 \\ -\ 1\ 4 \\ \hline \end{array}$$

3.
$$\begin{array}{r} 5\ 2\cancel{c} \\ -\ 1\ 8\cancel{c} \\ \hline \end{array}$$

4.
$$\begin{array}{r} 9\ 5\cancel{c} \\ -\ 4\ 2\cancel{c} \\ \hline \end{array}$$

Name_____

Regroup a ten.

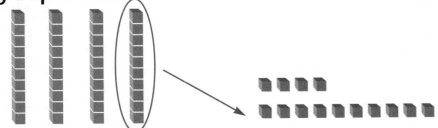

Take apart **1** ten to make
10 ones. **3** tens are left.

$10 + 4 = 14$ ones

T	O
$\overset{3}{\cancel{4}}$	$\overset{14}{\cancel{4}}$
–	5
3	9

Subtract.

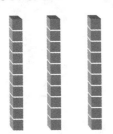

Subtract. Start with the ones.

1.

T	O
$\overset{7}{\cancel{8}}$	$\overset{14}{\cancel{4}}$
–	8
7	6

T	O
3	3
–	7

T	O
9	4
–	6

T	O
7	4
–	6

2.

T	O
6	4
–	9

T	O
2	4
–	7

T	O
8	3
–	5

T	O
4	4
–	9

3.

T	O
7	4
–	7

T	O
6	4
–	5

T	O
5	4
–	8

T	O
6	3
–	8

Unit 7 • Lesson 7

Subtract.

4.

T	O
²3̶	¹³3̶
−	5
2	8

T	O
⁵6̶	¹⁴4̶
−	6

T	O
²3̶	¹⁴4̶
−	7

T	O
⁸9̶	¹⁴4̶
−	5

T	O
5	2
−	7

5.

T	O
4	2
−	6

T	O
7	4
−	9

T	O
6	4
−	8

T	O
7	1
−	5

T	O
8	4
−	9

6.

$$34 - 8 \qquad 94 - 7 \qquad 74 - 5 \qquad 91 - 7 \qquad 23 - 6 \qquad 63 - 9 \qquad 54 - 6$$

Problem Solving Reasoning

Use mental math. Count back 1, 2, or 3 to find the difference.

7.

$$54 - 3 \qquad 63 - 2 \qquad 44 - 1 \qquad 73 - 1 \qquad 34 - 2 \qquad 23 - 3$$

★ **Test Prep**

Solve. Mark the space for your answer.
If the answer is **not here**, mark the space for **NH**.

8

$$\begin{array}{r} 63 \\ -9 \\ \hline \square \end{array}$$

44 ○   54 ○   55 ○   64 ○   NH ○

180 (one hundred eighty)

Unit 7 • Lesson 7

Name _____

Regroup a ten.

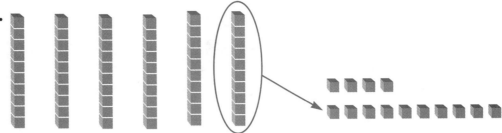

Take apart **1** ten to make **10** ones.
5 tens are left.

$10 + 4 = 14$ ones

T	O
$\overset{5}{\cancel{6}}$	$\overset{14}{4}$
$-\ 3$	7
2	7

Subtract.

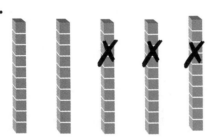

___

Subtract. Start with the ones.

1.

T	O
$\overset{3}{\cancel{4}}$	$\overset{13}{3}$
$-\ 2$	5
1	8

T	O
6	4
$-\ 1$	5

T	O
5	4
$-\ 1$	8

T	O
6	3
$-\ 2$	4

2.

T	O
6	4
$-\ 2$	7

T	O
4	3
$-\ 1$	9

T	O
9	4
$-\ 5$	9

T	O
6	3
$-\ 4$	4

3.

T	O
5	3
$-\ 2$	9

T	O
7	4
$-\ 5$	9

T	O
8	3
$-\ 2$	7

T	O
3	3
$-\ 1$	8

Subtract.

4.
34	63	94	73	34	93
− 15	− 24	− 68	− 56	− 19	− 65
19					

5.
| 93 | 80 | 73 | 34 | 73 | 44 |
| − 19 | − 17 | − 56 | − 19 | − 57 | −28 |

6.
| 54 | 63 | 84 | 63 | 34 | 83 |
| − 26 | − 29 | − 18 | − 28 | − 17 | − 65 |

Problem Solving Reasoning

Solve. Use any strategy.

7. There are **54** pigs. **28** pigs are playing in the mud. How many pigs are not playing in the mud?

8. There are **23** horses. **17** horses are out in the field. How many horses are still in the stables?

_____ pigs

_____ horses

★ Test Prep

Solve. Mark the space for your answer.
If the answer is **not here**, mark the space for **NH**.

| 84 |
| −37 |
| ☐ |

47 ○   48 ○   57 ○   58 ○   NH ○

Name _____

Use the table.
Solve.

Books Seen at the Book Fair

Student	Number of Books
Kyle	24
Yoko	43
Cheryl	31
Evan	40

1. How many more books does Evan see than Kyle?

   Think How many books does Evan see? __40__

   How many books does Kyle see? __24__

   Answer Evan sees __16__ more books than Kyle.

2. How many more books does Yoko see than Kyle?

   Think How many books does Yoko see? _____

   How many books does Kyle see? _____

   Answer Yoko sees _____ more books than Kyle.

3. How many books do Yoko and Cheryl see together?

   Think How many books does Yoko see? _____

   How many books does Cheryl see? _____

   Answer Yoko and Cheryl see _____ books.

Unit 7 • Lesson 9   (one hundred eighty-three) 183

Use the table. Solve.

Things Collected

Grade	Bottles	Cans
Second Grade	90	49
Third Grade	72	64

4. How many more bottles does the Second Grade collect than the Third Grade?

         Answer The Second Grade collects _____ more bottles.

5. How many fewer cans does the Second Grade collect than the Third Grade?

         Answer The Second Grade collects _____ fewer cans.

6. How many more bottles than cans does the Third Grade collect?

         Answer The Third Grade collects _____ more bottles than cans.

Extend Your Thinking

7. Write your own question about the table.
   Ask a friend to answer it. _____

   _____

   _____

   _____

Name _____

Regroup a ten.

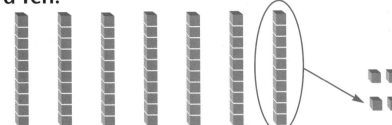

Take apart **1** ten to make **10** ones.
6 tens are left.

10 + 6 = 16 ones

Subtract.

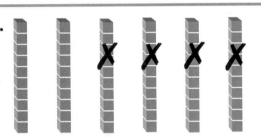

```
    T | O
    6 | 16
    7 | 6
 -  4 | 7
 -----------
    2 | 9
```

Subtract. Remember to regroup.

1.
```
   T | O
   3 | 16
   4 | 6
 - 2 | 7
 -------
   1 | 9
```
```
  T | O
  6 | 5
- 2 | 9
```
```
  T | O
  9 | 6
-   | 7
```
```
  T | O
  5 | 5
-   | 9
```

2.
```
  T | O
  6 | 6
-   | 9
```
```
  T | O
  4 | 6
- 1 | 7
```
```
  T | O
  8 | 6
- 5 | 9
```
```
  T | O
  7 | 5
-   | 9
```

3.
```
  T | O
  4 | 6
- 2 | 7
```
```
  T | O
  3 | 5
-   | 7
```
```
  T | O
  6 | 6
- 4 | 8
```
```
  T | O
  7 | 5
- 6 | 8
```

Subtract. Start with the ones.

4.
$$\begin{array}{r} 75 \\ -\ 29 \\ \hline 46 \end{array}$$
$$\begin{array}{r} 85 \\ -\ 7 \\ \hline \end{array}$$
$$\begin{array}{r} 56 \\ -\ 37 \\ \hline \end{array}$$
$$\begin{array}{r} 96 \\ -\ 7 \\ \hline \end{array}$$
$$\begin{array}{r} 86 \\ -\ 59 \\ \hline \end{array}$$

5.
$$\begin{array}{r} 96 \\ -\ 57 \\ \hline \end{array}$$
$$\begin{array}{r} 45 \\ -\ 27 \\ \hline \end{array}$$
$$\begin{array}{r} 66 \\ -\ 9 \\ \hline \end{array}$$
$$\begin{array}{r} 45 \\ -\ 18 \\ \hline \end{array}$$
$$\begin{array}{r} 96 \\ -\ 77 \\ \hline \end{array}$$

6.
$$\begin{array}{r} 75 \\ -\ 19 \\ \hline \end{array}$$
$$\begin{array}{r} 42 \\ -\ 19 \\ \hline \end{array}$$
$$\begin{array}{r} 95 \\ -\ 28 \\ \hline \end{array}$$
$$\begin{array}{r} 86 \\ -\ 8 \\ \hline \end{array}$$
$$\begin{array}{r} 71 \\ -\ 58 \\ \hline \end{array}$$

✓ Quick Check

Subtract.

1.
$$\begin{array}{r} 54 \\ -\ 8 \\ \hline \end{array}$$

2.
$$\begin{array}{r} 93 \\ -\ 37 \\ \hline \end{array}$$

3.
$$\begin{array}{r} 85 \\ -\ 19 \\ \hline \end{array}$$

4.
$$\begin{array}{r} 76 \\ -\ 47 \\ \hline \end{array}$$

186 (one hundred eighty-six)

Unit 7 • Lesson 10

Name _____

Subtract. Start with the ones.

1.
T	O
⁶7̷	¹⁷7̷
− 2	9
	8

T	O
⁸9̷	¹⁸8̷
− 6	9

T	O
⁷8̷	¹⁷7̷
− 1	8

T	O
⁴5̷	¹⁸8̷
−	9

2.
T	O
4	7
− 2	8

T	O
6	8
− 2	9

T	O
9	7
−	8

T	O
9	8
− 7	9

3.
T	O
4	8
− 2	9

T	O
6	7
− 3	8

T	O
5	8
− 1	9

T	O
4	7
−	9

4.
T	O
3	7
−	8

T	O
7	8
− 2	9

T	O
5	7
− 2	8

T	O
9	8
− 5	9

5.
T	O
8	8
− 6	9

T	O
5	7
− 3	8

T	O
7	8
−	9

T	O
6	7
− 3	9

Unit 7 • Lesson 11

Subtract.

6.
$$\begin{array}{r} 77 \\ -\ 9 \\ \hline 68 \end{array}$$
$$\begin{array}{r} 58 \\ -39 \\ \hline \end{array}$$
$$\begin{array}{r} 97 \\ -18 \\ \hline \end{array}$$
$$\begin{array}{r} 67 \\ -38 \\ \hline \end{array}$$
$$\begin{array}{r} 40 \\ -18 \\ \hline \end{array}$$

7.
$$\begin{array}{r} 98 \\ -69 \\ \hline \end{array}$$
$$\begin{array}{r} 47 \\ -28 \\ \hline \end{array}$$
$$\begin{array}{r} 98 \\ -\ 9 \\ \hline \end{array}$$
$$\begin{array}{r} 58 \\ -19 \\ \hline \end{array}$$
$$\begin{array}{r} 88 \\ -19 \\ \hline \end{array}$$

8.
$$\begin{array}{r} 87 \\ -18 \\ \hline \end{array}$$
$$\begin{array}{r} 68 \\ -29 \\ \hline \end{array}$$
$$\begin{array}{r} 48 \\ -\ 9 \\ \hline \end{array}$$
$$\begin{array}{r} 47 \\ -29 \\ \hline \end{array}$$
$$\begin{array}{r} 50 \\ -39 \\ \hline \end{array}$$

Problem Solving Reasoning Solve. Use any strategy.

9. Mario sees **48** red barns. Julie sees **29** white barns. How many more barns does Mario see?

_____ more barns

10. Julie sees **87** green tractors. Mario sees **58** white tractors. How many more tractors does Julie see?

_____ more tractors

★ Test Prep

Solve. Mark the space for your answer.
If the answer is **not here**, mark the space for **NH**.

$$\begin{array}{r} 88 \\ -29 \\ \hline \boxed{} \end{array}$$

58	59	68	69	NH
○	○	○	○	○

You can check subtraction by adding.

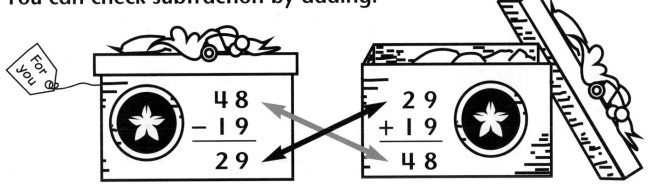

$$\begin{array}{r} 4\ 8 \\ -\ 1\ 9 \\ \hline 2\ 9 \end{array} \qquad \begin{array}{r} 2\ 9 \\ +\ 1\ 9 \\ \hline 4\ 8 \end{array}$$

Subtract. Check by adding.

1.
$$\begin{array}{r} 3\ 2 \\ -\ 1\ 9 \\ \hline 1\ 3 \end{array} \qquad \begin{array}{r} 1\ 3 \\ +\ 1\ 9 \\ \hline 3\ 2 \end{array}$$

2.
$$\begin{array}{r} 7\ 1 \\ -\ 2\ 8 \\ \hline \end{array} \qquad +\ \underline{\quad}$$

3.
$$\begin{array}{r} 4\ 2 \\ -\ 1\ 5 \\ \hline \end{array} \qquad +\ \underline{\quad}$$

4.
$$\begin{array}{r} 7\ 2 \\ -\ 4\ 8 \\ \hline \end{array} \qquad +\ \underline{\quad}$$

5.
$$\begin{array}{r} 8\ 1 \\ -\ 2\ 6 \\ \hline \end{array} \qquad +\ \underline{\quad}$$

6.
$$\begin{array}{r} 9\ 2 \\ -\ 6\ 4 \\ \hline \end{array} \qquad +\ \underline{\quad}$$

7.
$$\begin{array}{r} 8\ 1 \\ -\ 2\ 8 \\ \hline \end{array} \qquad +\ \underline{\quad}$$

8.
$$\begin{array}{r} 9\ 2 \\ -\ 7\ 3 \\ \hline \end{array} \qquad +\ \underline{\quad}$$

9.
$$\begin{array}{r} 9\ 2 \\ -\ 2\ 3 \\ \hline \end{array} \qquad +\ \underline{\quad}$$

10.
$$\begin{array}{r} 9\ 1 \\ -\ 6\ 3 \\ \hline \end{array} \qquad +\ \underline{\quad}$$

11.
$$\begin{array}{r} 3\ 2 \\ -\ 1\ 9 \\ \hline \end{array} \qquad +\ \underline{\quad}$$

12.
$$\begin{array}{r} 8\ 1 \\ -\ 6\ 6 \\ \hline \end{array} \qquad +\ \underline{\quad}$$

13.
$$\begin{array}{r} 6\ 2 \\ -\ 4\ 8 \\ \hline \end{array} \qquad +\ \underline{\quad}$$

14.
$$\begin{array}{r} 8\ 1 \\ -\ 6\ 3 \\ \hline \end{array} \qquad +\ \underline{\quad}$$

15.
$$\begin{array}{r} 5\ 2 \\ -\ 1\ 8 \\ \hline \end{array} \qquad +\ \underline{\quad}$$

Subtract. Check by adding.

16.
$$68$$
$$-42$$
$+$ _____

17.
$$40$$
$$-15$$
$+$ _____

18.
$$54$$
$$-19$$
$+$ _____

19.
$$51$$
$$-18$$
$+$ _____

20.
$$73$$
$$-28$$
$+$ _____

21.
$$76$$
$$-25$$
$+$ _____

22.
$$32$$
$$-19$$
$+$ _____

23.
$$61$$
$$-33$$
$+$ _____

24.
$$85$$
$$-27$$
$+$ _____

25.
$$49$$
$$-18$$
$+$ _____

26.
$$56$$
$$-19$$
$+$ _____

27.
$$42$$
$$-24$$
$+$ _____

28.
$$75$$
$$-26$$
$+$ _____

29.
$$72$$
$$-44$$
$+$ _____

30.
$$74$$
$$-19$$
$+$ _____

**Problem Solving
Reasoning**

31. How does adding help you check your subtraction?

_____

★ Test Prep

Solve. Mark the space for your answer.
If the answer is **not here**, mark the space for **NH**.

32

$$83$$
$$-25$$
$$\overline{58}$$

$$\Box$$
$$+25$$
$$\overline{83}$$

25	48	58	83	NH
○	○	○	○	○

190 (one hundred ninety)

You can rewrite the problem to find the sum.

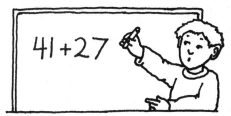

Rewrite the problem. Find the sum or difference.

1.
28 + 25

$$\begin{array}{r} 1 \\ 2\,8 \\ +2\,5 \\ \hline 5\,3 \end{array}$$

2.
54 − 38

$$\begin{array}{r} 5\,4 \\ -3\,8 \\ \hline \end{array}$$

3.
56 + 36

4.
46 + 32

5.
53 − 19

6.
52 − 49

Solve.

Work Space

7. 32 + 57 = ____

8. 53 − 19 = ____

9. 38 + 38 = ____

Rewrite the problem. Solve.

10.

25 + 16	25 − 16
$$\begin{array}{r} 1 \\ 25 \\ +16 \\ \hline 41 \end{array}$$	

11.

58 + 27	58 − 27

12.

69 + 19	69 − 19

13.

48 + 36	48 − 36

☑ Quick Check

Solve.

1. $$\begin{array}{r} 62 \\ -\ 7 \\ \hline \end{array}$$
2. $$\begin{array}{r} 86 \\ -38 \\ \hline \end{array}$$

Subtract. Check by adding.

3. $$\begin{array}{r} 44 \\ -29 \\ \hline \end{array}$$ $$+ \underline{\quad}$$
4. $$\begin{array}{r} 62 \\ -37 \\ \hline \end{array}$$ $$+ \underline{\quad}$$

Rewrite the problem. Solve.

5. 67 − 29

Name _____

Problem

Valerie's house is **57** miles away from the beach.
Nico's house is **38** miles away from the beach.
How much farther away is Valerie's house than Nico's house from the beach?

1 Understand

I need to find out how much farther Valerie's house is from the beach than Nico's house.

2 Decide

Can I use simpler numbers to help?
Have I solved any problems like this before?

3 Solve

If I use simpler numbers, the problem would read:
Valerie's house is **60** miles away from the beach.
Nico's house is **40** miles away from the beach.
How much farther away is Valerie's house from the beach?

I will subtract to find about how much farther it is.
60 − 40 = 20
I think it is about 20 miles farther away.

Now I will subtract the actual amounts.

$$\begin{array}{r} 57 \\ -\ 38 \\ \hline 19 \end{array}$$

Answer It is **19** miles farther away.

4 Look back

Is my answer reasonable? Why or why not?

Unit 7 • Lesson 14   (one hundred ninety-three) 193

Solve. Use simpler numbers or other strategies. Show your work.

1. Jenna jumps rope **67** times on Monday. She jumps rope **49** times on Tuesday. How many more times does she jump rope on Monday?

   Work Space

   Answer _____ more times

2. Kirk has to read **46** pages in his chapter book. He reads **38** pages. How many pages does Kirk have left to read?

   Work Space

   Answer _____ pages

3. Tanya uses a magnet to pick up paper clips. The first time she picks up **63** paper clips. The second time she picks up **47** paper clips. How many more paper clips does she pick up the first time?

   Work Space

   Answer _____ more paper clips

4. Raphael and his aunt go apple picking. Together their apples weigh **62** pounds. His aunt's apples weigh **43** pounds. How much do Raphael's apples weigh?

   Work Space

   Answer _____ pounds

Subtract.

1. **6** tens − **4** tens = _____ tens

   60 − 40 = ____

2. **8** tens − **3** tens = _____ tens

   80 − 30 = ____

3.   **55 − 25 = ____**

4.   **75 − 30 = ____**

Subtract.

5. **3 6**
    −   9

6. **5 8**
    − 4 9

7. **2 1**
    −   8

8. **6 8¢**
    − 4 2¢

9. **3 7**
    − 2 8

10. **6 4**
    −   7

11. **9 2¢**
    − 7 3¢

12. **7 1**
    − 2 9

13. **3 8**
    − 1 7

14. **7 2**
    − 3 9

15. **8 4**
    − 4 7

16. **3 0**
    −   8

17. **5 2**
    − 3 4

18. **9 1**
    −   6

19. **5 6¢**
    − 2 7¢

Problem Solving Reasoning Use the table. Solve.

Cracker Boxes Sold

	Monday	Tuesday
Room 5	30	31
Room 6	29	28

20. How many boxes of crackers were sold on Monday?

    _____ boxes

21. How many more boxes of crackers did Room 5 sell on Tuesday than Room 6?

    _____ more boxes

Name_____

1

8, 7, 15 | ○ 8 + 8 = 16   ○ 15 − 7 = 8
              ○ 9 + 7 = 16   ○ 16 − 8 = 8

2

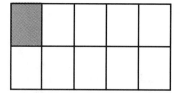 | $\frac{1}{5}$ $\frac{1}{8}$ $\frac{1}{10}$ $\frac{1}{12}$
                          ○   ○   ○   ○

3

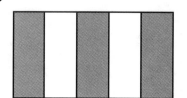 | $\frac{1}{5}$ $\frac{3}{5}$ $\frac{4}{5}$ $\frac{5}{5}$
                          ○   ○   ○   ○

Solve.

4

25 + 35 = ☐ | 50   55   60   70   NH
                 ○   ○   ○   ○   ○

5

80 − 30 = ☐ | 70   60   55   40   NH
                 ○   ○   ○   ○   ○

6

  34
+ 14
☐ | 38   44   48   58   NH
               ○   ○   ○   ○   ○

7

  27
+ 48
☐ | 65   75   76   86   NH
               ○   ○   ○   ○   ○

8

  49
− 28
☐ | 31   29   21   11   NH
               ○   ○   ○   ○   ○

9

  82
− 64
☐ | 28   27   18   17   NH
               ○   ○   ○   ○   ○

196 (one hundred ninety-six)

Unit 7 • Cumulative Review

UNIT 8 • TABLE OF CONTENTS

Time and Money

Dear Family,

During the next few weeks our math class will be learning about time and money.

You can expect to see homework that provides practice with reading and writing time. There will also be homework that provides practice with counting combinations of coins.

As we learn about time and money, you may wish to keep the following sample as a guide.

10 o'clock
10:00

half past 8
8:30

quarter past 4
4:15

quarter to 2
1:45

Sincerely,

Write the time.

1.

 o'clock

2.

_____ o'clock

2:00

3.

_____ o'clock

4:00

4.

_____ o'clock

6:00

5.

_____ o'clock

9:00

6.

_____ o'clock

12:00

What time does the clock show?

7.

___9___ o'clock

___9:00___

8.

_____ o'clock

_____:_____

9.

_____ o'clock

_____:_____

10.

_____ o'clock

_____:_____

11.

_____ o'clock

_____:_____

12.

_____ o'clock

_____:_____

13.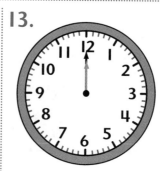

_____ o'clock

_____:_____

14.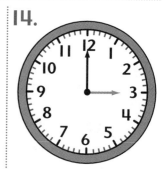

_____ o'clock

_____:_____

★ Test Prep

Give the time. Mark the space for your answer.

15

12:00	2:00	4:00	5:00
○	○	○	○

Tell the time two ways.

1.

half past ___4___

___4:30___

2.

half past _____

____:____

3.

half past _____

____:____

4.

half past _____

____:____

5.

half past _____

____:____

6.

half past _____

____:____

7.

half past _____

____:____

8.

half past _____

____:____

9.

half past _____

____:____

Show the time on the clock. Draw the hands.

10.

half past **2**

11.

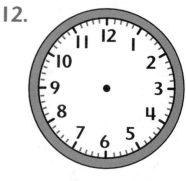

half past **4**

12.

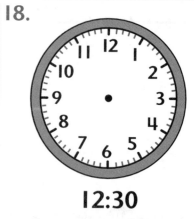

half past **6**

13.

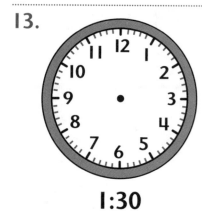

1:30

14.

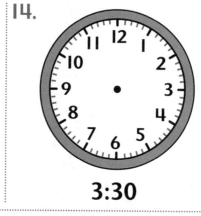

3:30

15.

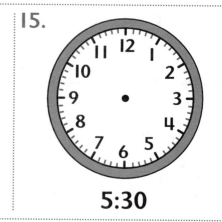

5:30

16.

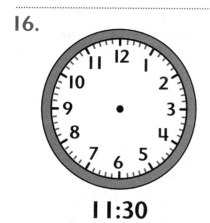

11:30

17.

10:30

18.

12:30

★ Test Prep

Give the time. Mark the space for your answer.

19

7:30	6:45	8:30	6:30
○	○	○	○

202 (two hundred two)

Unit 8 • Lesson 2

This clock shows
15 minutes after 12
or
12:15.

Write the time.

1.

1:15

2.

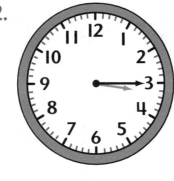

____:____

3.

____:____

4.

____:____

5.

____:____

6.

____:____

15 minutes after 2
is the same as
quarter past 2
or
2:15.

Show the time. Draw the hands.

7.   **6:15**

quarter past **6**

8.   **8:15**

quarter past **8**

9.   **10:15**

quarter past **10**

 Quick Check

Write the time.

1.

_____ o'clock

2.

_____ : _____

Match.

3. quarter past **1**   5:15

   quarter past **3**   1:15

   quarter past **5**   3:15

This clock shows
45 minutes after 11
or
11:45.

Write the time.

1.

7:45

2.

___:___

3.

___:___

4.

___:___

5.

___:___

6.

___:___

45 minutes after 2
is the same as
quarter to 3
or
2:45.

Show the time. Draw the hands.

7. **8:45**

quarter to **9**

8. **5:45**

quarter to **6**

9. **9:45**

quarter to **10**

Problem Solving
Reasoning

10. If the hour hand is pointing to just before the **3**, and the minute hand is pointing to the **9**, what time is it? How do you know?

_____

_____

_____

★ Test Prep

Which is the same? Mark the space for your answer.

11

quarter to **2**

11:45	12:45	1:45	2:45
○	○	○	○

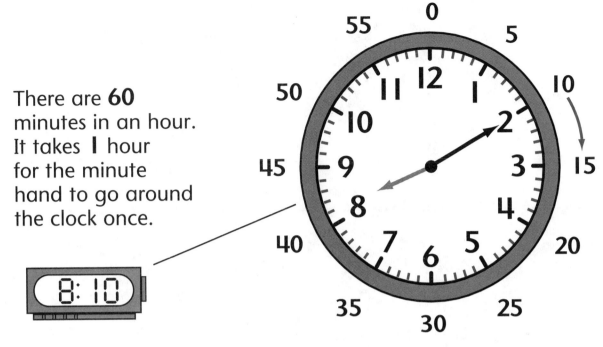

There are **60** minutes in an hour. It takes **1** hour for the minute hand to go around the clock once.

There are **60** seconds in a minute. It takes **5** minutes for the minute hand to go from number to number.

Match.

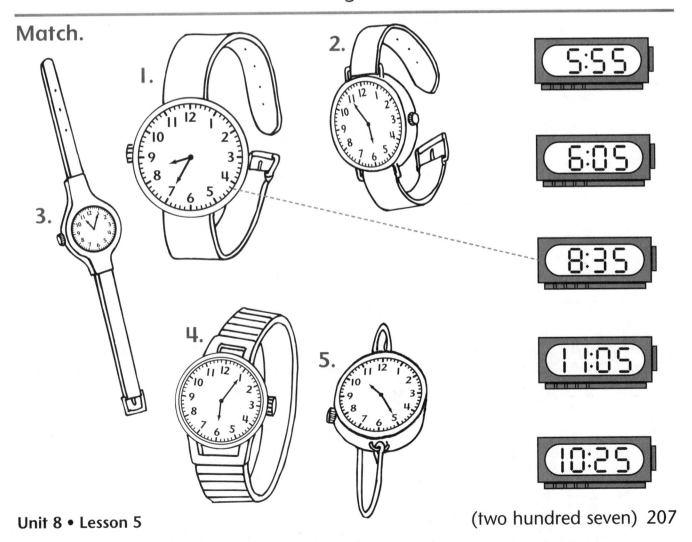

1.
2.
3.
4.
5.

5:55

6:05

8:35

11:05

10:25

Unit 8 • Lesson 5

(two hundred seven) 207

40 minutes after 5
is the same as
twenty to 6
or
5:40.

Count by 5's. Write the time.

6.

3:35

7.

_____ : _____

8.

_____ : _____

9.

_____ : _____

Problem Solving
Reasoning

10. Write or draw what you can do in a minute.

★ **Test Prep**

Which is the same? Mark the space for your answer.

11

twenty to **10**

10:40	9:30	9:40	10:20
○	○	○	○

There are **24** hours in a day.
The hour hand goes around the clock
two times each day.

I day

12 A.M.
midnight

12 P.M.
noon

12 A.M.
midnight

The hours from
midnight to noon
are labeled A.M.

The hours from
noon to midnight
are labeled P.M.

6:00 A.M.
is in the morning.

6:00 P.M.
is in the evening.

Write the time. Solve.

1. Renee was at school from

   to

8:00 A.M.   2:00 P.M.

She was at school for __6__ hours.

Write the time. Solve.

2. Renee did homework from

 to

_____ **:** _____ **P.M.**   _____ **:** _____ **P.M.**

She did homework for ____ hour and _____ minutes.

---

3. Renee watched T.V. from

 to

_____ **:** _____ **P.M.**   _____ **:** _____ **P.M.**

She watched T.V. for _____ minutes.

✓ Quick Check

Write the time.

1.    **2.**

_____ **:** _____   _____ **:** _____

---

3. Stephen played from

 to

_____ **:** _____ **A.M.**   _____ **:** _____ **P.M.**

He played for ____ hours and _____ minutes.

Unit 8 • Lesson 6

Name _____

**Problem Solving Application:
Use a Schedule**

Problem Solving Plan
1. Understand   2. Decide   3. Solve   4. Look back

Eric's Saturday Plan

7:30 A.M.	Wake up
8:00 A.M.	Eat breakfast
8:30 A.M.	Clean room
9:00 A.M.	Go to Nathan's house
12:00 P.M.	Go home and have lunch
1:30 P.M.	Go to club meeting
3:30 P.M.	Play soccer
6:00 P.M.	Eat supper
7:00 P.M.	Watch T.V.
8:45 P.M.	Go to sleep

Use the schedule. Solve.

1. What time will Eric eat breakfast?
   Think Find Eat breakfast on the schedule.
         Follow across to the time.

   Answer _____ 8:00 A.M. _____

2. What will Eric do at **9:00** A.M.?
   Think Find **9:00** A.M. on the schedule.
         Follow across.

   Answer _____

3. What time will Eric go to sleep?
   Think Find Go to sleep on the schedule.
         Follow across to the time.

   Answer _____

Unit 8 • Lesson 7

(two hundred eleven) 211

Eric's Saturday Plan

7:30 A.M.	Wake up
8:00 A.M.	Eat breakfast
8:30 A.M.	Clean room
9:00 A.M.	Go to Nathan's house
12:00 P.M.	Go home and have lunch
1:30 P.M.	Go to club meeting
3:30 P.M.	Play soccer
6:00 P.M.	Eat supper
7:00 P.M.	Watch T.V.
8:45 P.M.	Go to sleep

Use the schedule. Solve.

4. What will Eric do at **8:30** A.M.?

   Answer _____

5. What time will Eric go home for lunch?

   Answer _____

6. What will Eric do just after lunch?

   Answer _____

Extend Your Thinking

7. Make up your own question about the schedule and show how you
   solve it. _____

   _____

   _____

Unit 8 • Lesson 7

Name _____   **Calendar**

Complete.

One Year

1.

January	February	March	April
1st _____	2nd _____	_____	_____
May	June	July	August
_____	_____	_____	_____
September	October	November	December
_____	_____	_____	_____

2. There are ___12___ months in a year.

The Months in One Year

January	_____	_____	_____
1st	2nd	3rd	4th
_____	_____	_____	_____
5th	6th	7th	8th
_____	_____	_____	_____
9th	10th	11th	12th

Unit 8 • Lesson 8

eleventh **11th**	twelfth **12th**	thirteenth **13th**	fourteenth **14th**	fifteenth **15th**
sixteenth **16th**	seventeenth **17th**	eighteenth **18th**	nineteenth **19th**	twentieth **20th**

Copy the calendar in your room.

3.

Sunday	Monday	Tuesday	Wednesday	Thursday	Friday	Saturday

Write how many.

4. Sundays _____   **5.** Tuesdays _____   **6.** Days in a week _____

7. What is the **fifteenth** day in this month? _____

8. What is the **twentieth** day in this month? _____

★ Test Prep

What day of the week is the **nineteenth**?

9

			January			
S	M	T	W	Th	F	S
					1	2
3	4	5	6	7	8	9
10	11	12	13	14	15	16
17	18	19	20	21	22	23
24	25	26	27	28	29	30
31						

○ Sunday   ○ Tuesday

○ Wednesday   ○ Friday

214 (two hundred fourteen)

Unit 8 • Lesson 8

Name _____

 **1** nickel
or
5 cents
5¢

 1 dime
or
10 cents
10¢

Count the money.

1.

__5__ ¢, __10__ ¢, __15__ ¢   __15__ ¢
                                   total

2.

_____ ¢, _____ ¢   _____ ¢
                        total

3.

_____ ¢, _____ ¢, _____ ¢, _____ ¢   _____ ¢
                                          total

4.

_____ ¢, _____ ¢, _____ ¢, _____ ¢, _____ ¢   _____ ¢
                                                   total

5.

_____ ¢, _____ ¢, _____ ¢, _____ ¢   _____ ¢
                                          total

Unit 8 • Lesson 9   (two hundred fifteen) 215

How much money?

6.   **Think**
10¢, 20¢

_____20_____ ¢

7.

_____ ¢

8.

_____ ¢

9.

_____ ¢

Problem Solving
Reasoning

10. If you have **4** dimes and **2** nickels, how much money do you have? How do you know?

_____

_____

_____

_____

★ Test Prep

How much money? Mark the space for your answer.

11

15¢	20¢	25¢	30¢
○	○	○	○

216 (two hundred sixteen)

Unit 8 • Lesson 9

Copyright © Houghton Mifflin Company. All rights reserved.

Name _____

Count by **10**'s.	Then count on by **5**'s.	Then count on by **1**'s.

10¢, 20¢, 30¢   35¢, 40¢, 45¢   46¢, 47¢, 48¢

Count. Write the total.

1.

_10_ ¢, _20_ ¢, _25_ ¢, _30_ ¢, _31_ ¢, _32_ ¢, _33_ ¢   _33_ ¢
                                                          total

2.

_____ ¢, _____ ¢, _____ ¢, _____ ¢, _____ ¢, _____ ¢, _____ ¢   _____ ¢
                                                                total

3.

_____ ¢, _____ ¢, _____ ¢, _____ ¢, _____ ¢, _____ ¢, _____ ¢   _____ ¢
                                                                total

4.

_____ ¢, _____ ¢, _____ ¢, _____ ¢, _____ ¢, _____ ¢, _____ ¢   _____ ¢
                                                                total

Unit 8 • Lesson 10

How much money?

5.

   Think
   10¢, 15¢, 16¢

   _____¢

6.

   _____¢

Write the amounts. Use >, <, or =.

7. **2** dimes = ___20___ ¢   **5** nickels = ___25___ ¢

   2 dimes (<) **5** nickels

8. **6** nickels = _____¢   **3** dimes = _____¢

   6 nickels ( ) **3** dimes

☑ Quick Check

Fill in the missing month.

1. October, _____ , December

How much money?

2.

   _____¢
   total

Use >, <, or =.

3. **4** dimes ( ) **6** nickels

218 (two hundred eighteen)

Unit 8 • Lesson 10

I quarter

25¢

I quarter

25¢

Count. Write the total.

1.

___25___ ¢, ___30___ ¢

___30___ ¢
total

2.

_____ ¢, _____ ¢, _____ ¢

_____ ¢
total

3.

_____ ¢, _____ ¢, _____ ¢, _____ ¢

_____ ¢
total

4.

_____ ¢, _____ ¢, _____ ¢

_____ ¢
total

How much money?

5.  **Think**
 25¢, 35¢, 36¢

_____ ¢

6.

_____ ¢

7.

_____ ¢

8.

_____ ¢

9.

_____ ¢

10.

_____ ¢

★ Test Prep

How much money? Mark the space for your answer.

11

36¢	40¢	46¢	29¢
○	○	○	○

220 (two hundred twenty)

Unit 8 • Lesson 11

Find the total cost. Ring the correct amount.

I.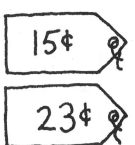

$$\begin{array}{r} 15¢ \\ + 23¢ \\ \hline 38¢ \end{array}$$

2.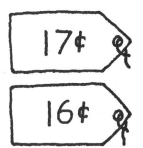

3.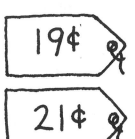

★ Test Prep

How much money? Mark the space for your answer.

4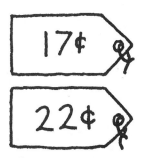

29¢   39¢   40¢   49¢
○   ○   ○   ○

How much change?

1. Elena had:

30¢

She bought:

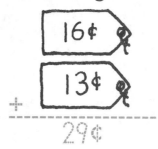

16¢

13¢

+ _ _ _ _ _ _ _ _ _

29¢

She got back:

30¢
−29¢
_____
1¢

---

2. Had: Bought: Got back:

25¢

15¢

7¢

+ _ _ _ _ _ _ _

22¢

3. Had: Bought: Got back:

40¢

24¢

8¢

☑ **Quick Check**

How much money?

1.

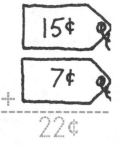

_____¢
total

Find the total cost.

2.

24¢

18¢

How much change?

3. Had: Bought: Got back:

45¢

14¢

22¢

Problem

Lee has a bag of nickels and dimes.
How many different ways can he pay for
a **45¢** pencil?

1 **Understand**

I need to find out how many different ways Lee can pay for a
45¢ pencil using only nickels and dimes.

2 **Decide**

I can make a list.

3 **Solve**

__4__ dimes and __1__ nickel
__3__ dimes and __3__ nickels
__2__ dimes and __5__ nickels
__1__ dime and __7__ nickels
__9__ nickels

There are __5__ different ways Lee can pay for a pencil worth **45¢**.

4 **Look back**

Did I find all the ways?

Make a list to solve.

1. Sari has pennies and nickels. How many different ways can she pay for a balloon that costs **17¢**?

   Sari can pay for the balloon _____ different ways.

2. Duncan has a box full of change. How many different ways can he pay for a whistle that costs **35¢**, using at least **1** quarter?

   Duncan can pay for the whistle _____ different ways.

3. Diane has a bag of pennies, nickels, and dimes. How many different ways can she buy a sticker worth **25¢**, using at least **1** dime?

   Diane can pay for the sticker _____ different ways.

224 (two hundred twenty-four)

Name _____

Show the time on the clock. Draw the hands.

1.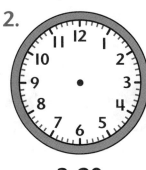

8:10

2.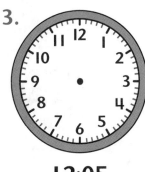

3:20

3.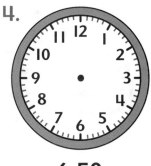

12:05

4.

6:50

Fill in the blank.

5. There are _____ minutes in **1** hour.

6. There are _____ days in **1** week.

7. There are **24** hours in **1** _____.

8. There are **12** _____ in **1** year.

Write the time. Solve.

9. Billy played the drums from

 to

___ : ___ P.M.   ___ : ___ P.M.

He played the drums for _____ minutes.

How much money?

10.

_____ ¢

11.

_____ ¢

12.

_____ ¢

Ring the correct amount.

13.

41¢

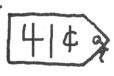

Write the amounts. Use >, <, or =.

14. **3** dimes = _____ ¢   **7** nickels = _____ ¢

3 dimes ◯ 7 nickels

15. **I** quarter = _____ ¢   **5** nickels = _____ ¢

I quarter ◯ 5 nickels

Problem Solving Reasoning **Make a list to solve.**

16. How many different ways can you make **30¢**, using only nickels and dimes?

_____ different ways

Unit 8 • Review

1

36	39	42		48	51

41   43   45   47
○   ○   ○   ○

2

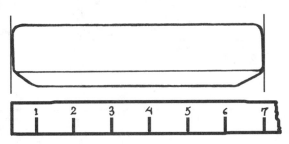

○   ○   ○   ○

3

5   6   7   8
○   ○   ○   ○

4

○ **10** o'clock

○ quarter to **3**

○ half past **3**

○ quarter past **10**

5

1 minute = _____ seconds

24   30   60   90
○   ○   ○   ○

6

○ **3** dimes < **6** nickels   ○ **2** dimes = **5** nickels

○ **4** dimes > **7** nickels   ○ **1** quarter > **3** dimes

Decide on an answer. Mark the space for your answer.
If the answer is **not here**, mark the space for **NH**.

 7

$8 + (4 + 4) =$ ☐

18	17	16	15	NH
○	○	○	○	○

8

○ 30¢
○ 25¢
○ 21¢
○ 15¢
○ NH

9

○ 42¢
○ 38¢
○ 33¢
○ 29¢
○ NH

10

$50 + 35 =$ ☐

75	80	85	90	NH
○	○	○	○	○

11

$90 - 25 =$ ☐

55	60	65	70	NH
○	○	○	○	○

12

```
   12
   35
 + 24
 ┌────┐
 └────┘
```

○ 81
○ 71
○ 69
○ 61
○ NH

13

```
   74
 − 29
 ┌────┐
 └────┘
```

○ 65
○ 55
○ 54
○ 45
○ NH

UNIT 9 • TABLE OF CONTENTS

Data and Probability

Dear Family,

During the next few weeks our math class will be learning about data and probability.

You can expect to see homework that provides practice with data and probability.

As we learn about probability, you may wish to keep the following sample as a guide.

This spinner will always stop on red.

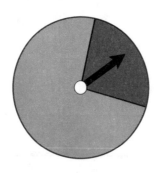

This spinner will sometimes stop on red.

This spinner will never stop on red.

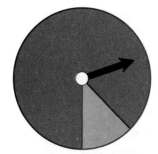

You are more likely to spin red on this spinner.

You are less likely to spin red on this spinner.

Sincerely,

Use the picture. Write the numbers.

1. There are ___5___ students reading.

2. There are _____ students writing.

3. There are _____ students in all.

4. There are _____ books on the top shelf.

5. There are _____ books on the middle shelf.

6. There are _____ books on the bottom shelf.

7. The top shelf has _____ more books than the bottom shelf.

8. There are _____ books in all.

9. What time does the clock say? ___ : ___

Look at the picture.
Cross out the objects in the picture as you complete the tally chart.
Remember that IIII stands for 5.

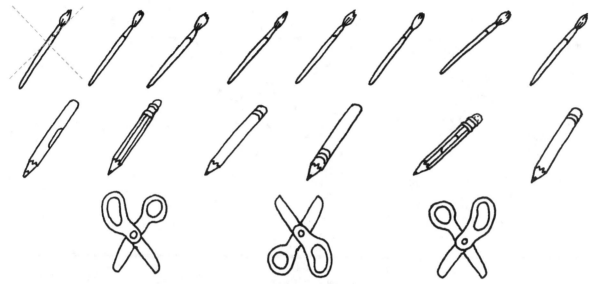

10.

Art Supplies	
 paintbrush	
 pencils	
 scissors	

Solve.

11. Are there more paintbrushes or scissors? _____

   How do you know? _____

   _____

★ Test Prep

Mark under the number of tallies shown.

12 IIII II | 4   5   6   7
                    ○   ○   ○   ○

232 (two hundred thirty-two)   Unit 9 • Lesson 1

Take a survey.

1. Ask 10 classmates to choose where they want to go on a field trip. Make tallies on the chart to record the data. Then write the total.

Field Trip Choices		
	Tally	**Total**
Farm		
Museum		
Factory		

Use the completed chart.

2. Which place do most of your classmates want to visit? _____

3. Which place was chosen the least? _____

Use your tally chart to complete the graph.
Fill in 1 box for every tally.

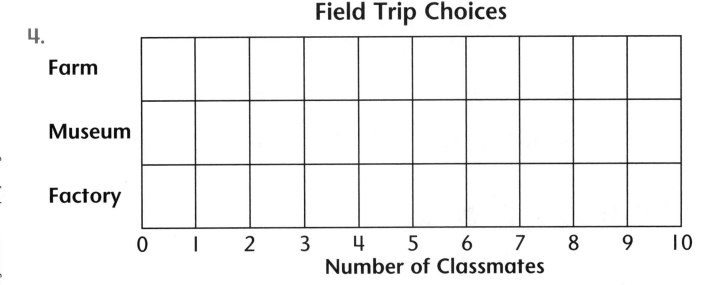

Field Trip Choices

4.

Take a survey.

5. Ask 15 classmates to choose their favorite school subject. Complete the tally chart.

Favorite Subjects		
	Tally	Total
Math		
Science		
Art		
Reading		

6. Which subject was chosen the most? _____

7. Which subject was chosen the least? _____

**Problem Solving
Reasoning**

8. Suppose you had asked all of your classmates to choose their favorite subject. Which subject do you think would be chosen the most? Why? _____

_____

_____

★ Test Prep

Which drink was chosen the least? Mark the space for your answer.

9

Favorite Drink	
Juice	IIII
Milk	HHT III
Lemonade	HHT I
Water	HHT

juice   milk   lemonade   water
○   ○   ○   ○

     Unit 9 • Lesson 2

Name_____

Look at the tally chart.
Use the data to complete the graph.

Hits During the Season					
Kim	ЖЖ	ЖЖ	ЖЖ	ЖЖ	ЖЖ
Troy	ЖЖ	ЖЖ	ЖЖ		
Lee	ЖЖ	ЖЖ	ЖЖ	ЖЖ	

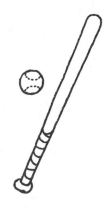

1.

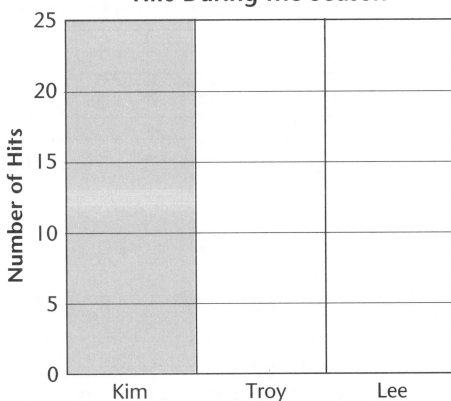

Hits During the Season

2. How many hits does Troy have? _____

3. Who has the most hits? _____

Complete the graph.

Sue Linn

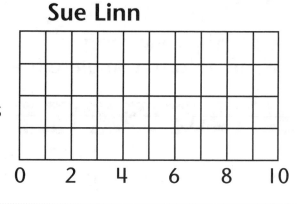

4. Sue Linn played
   10 games.
   She made **8** hits
   for her team.
   She struck out **6** times.
   She walked **4** times.

   Games
   Hits
   Strikeouts
   Walks

5. Jim played **9** games.
   He had **6** hits.
   He struck out **5** times.
   He walked **3** times.

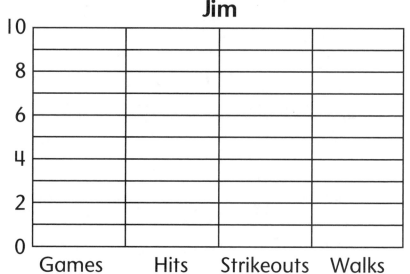

Jim

Problem Solving / Reasoning

6. Is it easier to see the information on the chart on page 235 or on the graph? Why? _____

 Quick Check

1. Mark the chart that shows the same information as the tally chart.

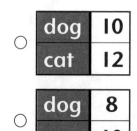

Favorite Pet	
dog	𝍱𝍱 II
cat	𝍱𝍱

○
dog	12
cat	10

○
dog	10
cat	12

○
dog	10
cat	8

○
dog	8
cat	10

236 (two hundred thirty-six)

Unit 9 • Lesson 3

The tally chart shows the ages of children at a day-care center.

Ages	Number of Children
1	||
2	|
3	||||
4	||
5	||||
6	|||

You can make a line plot of the data in the chart.
Add X's to show the ages of the children.

1.

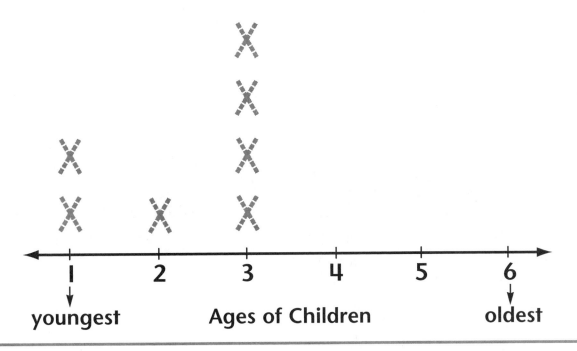

Count the X's to answer the questions.

2. How many children are **3** years old? _____

3. How many children are **6** years old? _____

The **range** is the difference between the youngest and the oldest age.

The **mode** is the age with the greatest number of X's.

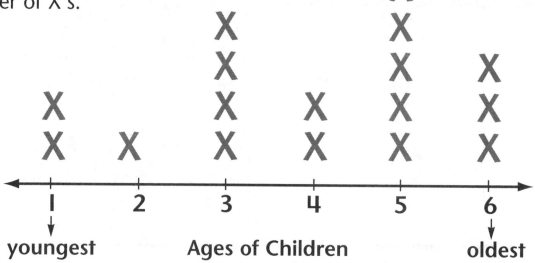

youngest   Ages of Children   oldest

Use the line plot.

4. What is the oldest age? _6_

5. What is the youngest age? ____

6. What is the range?

☐ – ☐ = ☐

     oldest age   youngest age   **range**

7. Which age has the greatest number of X's? ____?

                                                   mode

★ Test Prep

What is the number with the greatest number of X's? Mark under your answer.

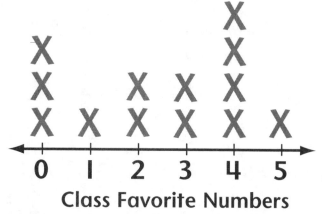

Class Favorite Numbers

5   4   3   2
○   ○   ○   ○

Favorite Book Characters

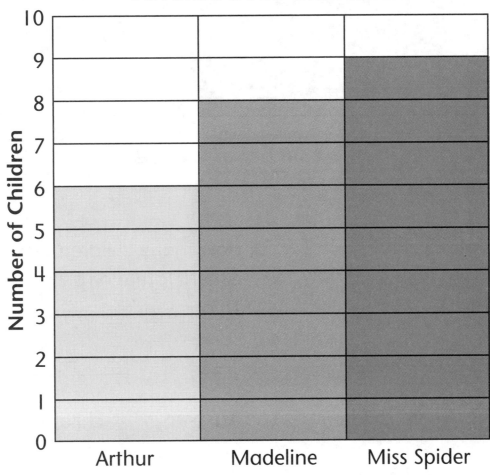

Use the graph.
Choose + or − to solve.

1. How many more children
pick Madeline than Arthur?

Think Do you add
or subtract? __subtract__

___8___ (−) ___6___ = ___2___

Answer __2__ more children

2. How many children pick
either Madeline or Miss Spider?

Think Do you add
or subtract? _____

___ ( ) ___ = ___

Answer ____ children

Favorite Book Themes

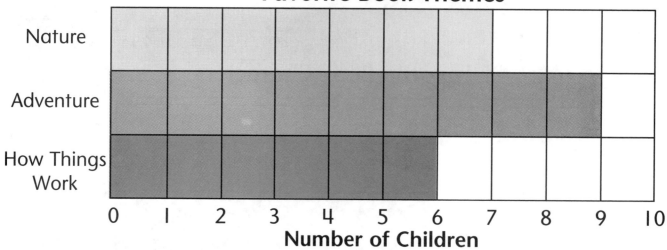

Number of Children

Use the graph.
Choose + or − to solve.

3. How many more children
pick Adventure than pick How
Things Work?

__9__ (−) __6__ = __3__

Answer __3__ more children

4. How many children pick
either Nature or pick How
Things Work?

____ ( ) ____ = ____

Answer ____ children

5. How many more children
pick Adventure than
Nature?

____ ( ) ____ = ____

Answer ____ more children

6. How many fewer children
pick How Things Work
than Nature?

____ ( ) ____ = ____

Answer ____ fewer children

Extend Your Thinking

7. How could you solve problem 3 another way?_____

_____

240 (two hundred forty)

Unit 9 • Lesson 5

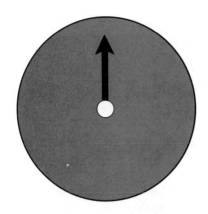

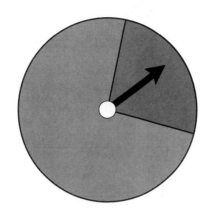

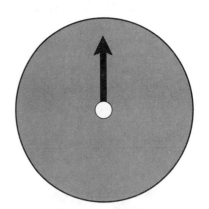

This spinner will **always** stop on red.

This spinner will **sometimes** stop on red.

This spinner will **never** stop on red.

Ring whether the spinner will sometimes, always, or never stop on gray.

1.

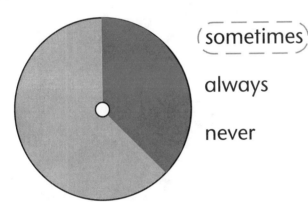

(sometimes)

always

never

2.

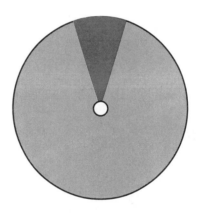

sometimes

always

never

3.

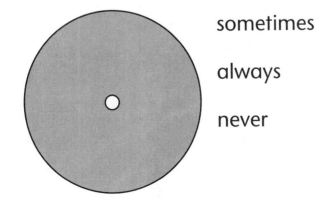

sometimes

always

never

4.

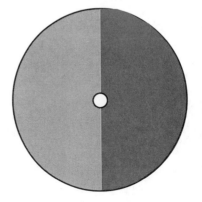

sometimes

always

never

Ring whether you would sometimes, always, or never pick a red marble from the bag.

5.

(sometimes)   always   never

6.

sometimes   always   never

7.

sometimes   always   never

8.

sometimes   always   never

★ **Test Prep**

Mark under the spinner that would never spin red.

9

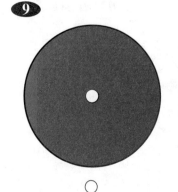   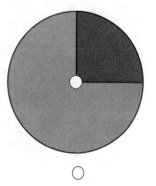   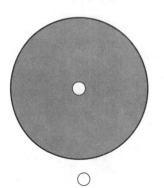   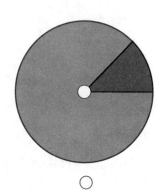

○   ○   ○   ○

242 (two hundred forty-two)

Name _____

Problem

Are you **more likely** or **less likely** to spin red?

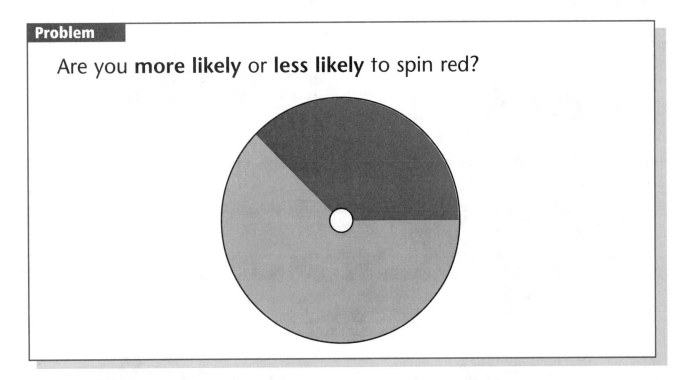

1 **Understand**

I need to predict whether I am more or less likely to stop on red.

2 **Decide**

I will use a paper clip to spin. I will spin 10 times and record my results in a table. Then I will predict.

3 **Solve**

Try it.

Spinner Results	
red	
gray	

Ring your prediction.   **Predict.**   more likely

(less likely)

4 **Look back**

Does the answer make sense?

Are you more likely or less likely to land on gray?
Use a paper clip. Spin 10 times and complete the table.
Ring your predictions.

1.

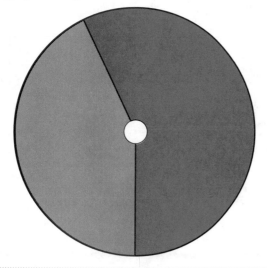

Spinner Results	
red	
gray	

Predict.   more likely

less likely

2.

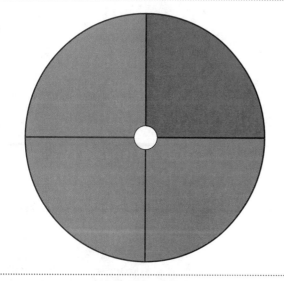

Spinner Results	
red	
gray	

Predict.   more likely

less likely

3.

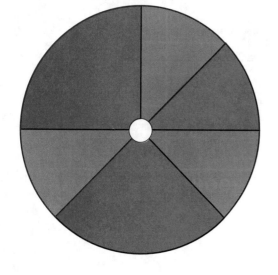

Spinner Results	
red	
gray	

Predict.   more likely

less likely

Name_____

Use the tally chart to complete the graph.
Answer the questions.

1.

Room 2's Favorite Fruit	
apples	⑷⑷
bananas	⑷⑷ ‖
grapes	⑷ ∣

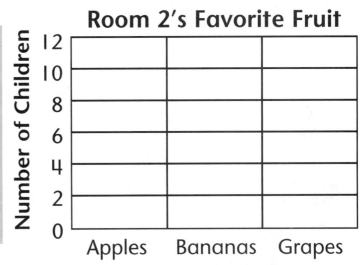

Room 2's Favorite Fruit

Number of Children

12
10
8
6
4
2
0

Apples   Bananas   Grapes

2. How many children chose apples? _____

3. Which fruit got the most votes? _____

___

Ring the answer.

4. Would you sometimes, always, or never pick a gray marble from the bag?

   sometimes

   always

   never

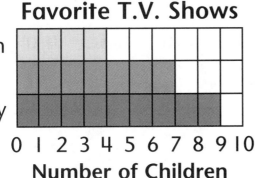

5. Are you more likely or less likely to land on red?

   more likely

   less likely

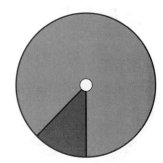

___

Problem Solving Reasoning Use the graph. Choose + or − to solve.

6.   **Favorite T.V. Shows**

Cartoon

Sports

Comedy

0 1 2 3 4 5 6 7 8 9 10
Number of Children

How many more children picked comedy than cartoon?

____ ◯ ____ = ____

____ more children.

1

$8 + 9 = 17$	$18 - 9 = 9$	$17 - 9 = 8$	$8 + 8 = 16$
○	○	○	○

2

○ **8** nickels = **4** dimes   ○ **1** quarter $<$ **3** dimes

○ **5** nickels = **1** quarter   ○ **6** nickels $>$ **3** dimes

3

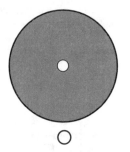 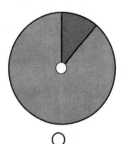 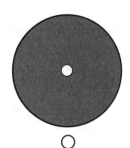 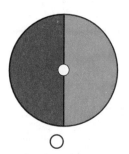

    ○   ○   ○   ○

Decide on an answer. Mark the space for your answer.
If the answer is **not here**, mark the space for **NH**.

4

$25 + 30 = \square$

45	60	55	50	NH
○	○	○	○	○

5

$90 - 35 = \square$

65	35	60	45	NH
○	○	○	○	○

6

33¢	38¢	48¢	43¢	NH
○	○	○	○	○

UNIT 10 • TABLE OF CONTENTS

Place Value to 1,000

Dear Family,

During the next few weeks our math class will be learning about place value to 1,000.

You can expect to see homework that provides practice with reading, writing, and comparing numbers through 1,000.

As we learn about place value you may wish to keep the following sample as a guide.

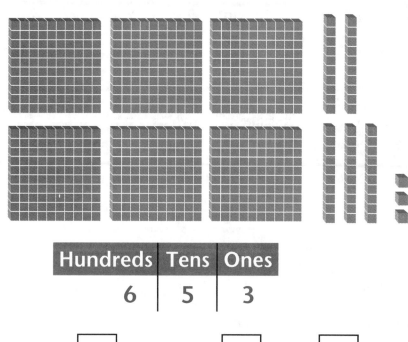

Hundreds	Tens	Ones
6	5	3

6 hundreds 5 tens 3 ones

or

600 + 50 + 3

= 653

Sincerely,

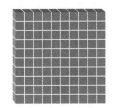

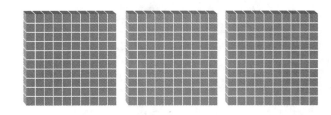

Hundreds	Tens	Ones
1	0	0

or

100

Hundreds	Tens	Ones
3	0	0

or

300

Count by 100's.

1. 100, _200_ , _____ , 400, _____ , 600, _____ , _____ , 900

2. _____ , 200, _____ , _____ , 500, _____ , _____ , 800, _____

Write the missing number.

3. | 200 | 300 | 400 |
   |-----|-----|-----|

4. | 300 | 400 | |
   |-----|-----|--|

5. | 400 | 500 | |
   |-----|-----|--|

6. | 500 | 600 | |
   |-----|-----|--|

7. | 600 | 700 | |
   |-----|-----|--|

8. | 700 | 800 | |
   |-----|-----|--|

Fill the blanks.

9. 100 is __1__ hundred __0__ tens __0__ ones.

10. 400 is ____ hundreds ____ tens ____ ones.

11. 600 is ____ hundreds ____ tens ____ ones.

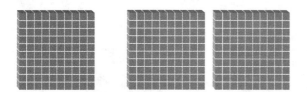

100 < 200
100 is less than **200**

200 > 100
200 is greater than **100**

Use > or < .

12. **100** ⓵ **300**

13. **500** ◯ **200**

14. **100** ◯ **400**

15. **400** ◯ **200**

16. **600** ◯ **100**

17. **300** ◯ **500**

Write the number.

18. **6** hundreds **0** tens **0** ones | 600

   4 hundreds **0** tens **0** ones |

   1 hundred **0** tens **0** ones |

   9 hundreds **0** tens **0** ones |

   5 hundreds **0** tens **0** ones |

Complete the table.

19.

	H	T	O
100	1	0	0
200			
300			
400			
500			

★ Test Prep

Decide on an answer. Mark the space for your answer.
If the answer is **not here**, mark the space for **NH**.

 20

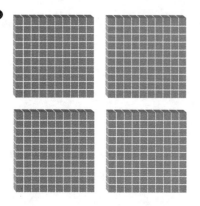

200	300	400	500	NH
◯	◯	◯	◯	◯

250 (two hundred fifty)

Complete.

1.

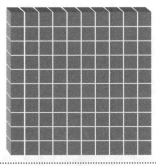

Hundreds	Tens	Ones
1	0	0

_100_

2.

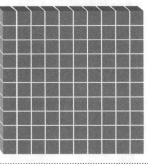

Hundreds	Tens	Ones

_____

3.

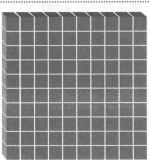

Hundreds	Tens	Ones

_____

Write the missing numbers.

4. 101, _102_ ,103, _____ , _____ ,106, _____ ,108, _____

5. 101,102, _____ , _____ , _____ , _____ , _____ , _____ ,109

Fill the blanks.

6. 102 is _1_ hundred _0_ tens _2_ ones, or _100_ + _0_ + _2_ .

7. 106 is ___ hundred ___ tens ___ ones, or ___ + ___ + ___ .

8. 109 is ___ hundred ___ tens ___ ones, or ___ + ___ + ___ .

9. 103 is ___ hundred ___ tens ___ ones, or ___ + ___ + ___ .

Fill in the blanks.

10. **107** is ____ hundred ____ tens ____ ones, or **100** + ____ + ____.

11. **101** is ____ hundred ____ tens ____ one , or _____ + ____ + ____.

12. **102** is ____ hundred ____ tens ____ ones, or _____ + ____ + ____.

13. **108** is ____ hundred ____ tens ____ ones, or _____ + ____ + ____.

14. **104** is ____ hundred ____ tens ____ ones, or _____ + ____ + ____.

15. **105** is ____ hundred ____ tens ____ ones, or _____ + ____ + ____.

Use > or <.

16. **104** (<) **106**

17. **105** ◯ **102**

18. **101** ◯ **100**

19. **105** ◯ **102**

20. **106** ◯ **105**

21. **102** ◯ **100**

22. **100** ◯ **102**

23. **109** ◯ **108**

24. **103** ◯ **101**

25. **108** ◯ **109**

26. **103** ◯ **102**

27. **105** ◯ **107**

Complete the number sentence.

28. 100 + 0 + 6 = | 106 |

29. 100 + 0 + 2 = | |

30. 100 + 0 + 9 = | |

31. 100 + 0 + 1 = | |

32. 100 + 0 + 7 = | |

33. 100 + 0 + 4 = | |

★ Test Prep

Mark which one is not true.

106 > 104   107 < 109   103 > 104   100 < 101
  ◯   ◯   ◯   ◯

Complete.

1.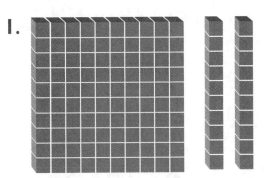

Hundreds	Tens	Ones
1	2	0

_100_ + _20_ + _0_

= _120_

2.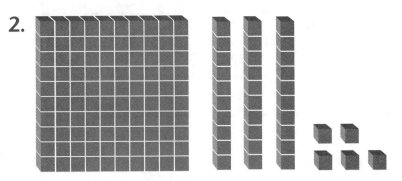

Hundreds	Tens	Ones

_____ + _____ + _____

= _____

Fill in the blanks.

3. I hundred **8** tens **5** ones is _185_ , or _100_ + _80_ + _5_.

4. I hundred **3** tens **4** ones is _____ , or _____ + _____ + _____.

5. I hundred **5** tens **9** ones is _____ , or _____ + _____ + _____.

Complete the number sentence.

6. 100 + 70 + 9 = $\boxed{179}$ 8. 100 + 30 + 6 = $\boxed{}$

7. 100 + 40 + 1 = $\boxed{}$ 9. 100 + 90 + 7 = $\boxed{}$

My **100** to **200** Chart

100	110	120	130	140	150	160	170	180	190
101	111	121	131	141	151	161	171	181	191
102	112	122	132	142	152	162	172	182	192
103	113	123	133	143	153	163	173	183	193
104	114	124	134	144	154	164	174	184	194
105	115	125	135	145	155	165	175	185	195
106	116	126	136	146	156	166	176	186	196
107	117	127	137	147	157	167	177	187	197
108	118	128	138	148	158	168	178	188	198
109	119	129	139	149	159	169	179	189	199
									200

Use > or < .

10. 134 ◯ 164

11. 141 ◯ 142

12. 127 ◯ 157

13. 159 ◯ 109

14. 172 ◯ 112

15. 199 ◯ 200

What comes

before?

16. _____ , 168

17. _____ , 180

between?

18. 145, _____ , 147

19. 198, _____ , 200

after?

20. 159, _____

21. 109, _____

✓ Quick Check

Write the missing numbers.

1.

100	200		400		600	700		

2. 103, _____ , 105 , _____ , _____ , 108

3. _____ , _____ , 189, _____ , 191

My **200** to **300** Chart

200	210	220	230	240	250	260	270	280	290
201	211	221	231	241	251	261	271	281	291
202	212	222	232	242	252	262	272	282	292
203	213	223	233	243	253	263	273	283	293
204	214	224	234	244	254	264	274	284	294
205	215	225	235	245	255	265	275	285	295
206	216	226	236	246	256	266	276	286	296
207	217	227	237	247	257	267	277	287	297
208	218	228	238	248	258	268	278	288	298
209	219	229	239	249	259	269	279	289	299
									300

Complete.

1. **226** is __2__ hundreds __2__ tens __6__ ones.

2. **241** is ____ hundreds ____ tens ____ one.

3. **201** is ____ hundreds ____ tens ____ one.

4. **210** is ____ hundreds ____ ten ____ ones.

5. **299** is ____ hundreds ____ tens ____ ones.

6. **300** is ____ hundreds ____ tens ____ ones.

H	T	O
2	2	6

7. **226** = __200__ + __20__ + __6__ ⟶

8. **241** = ____ + ____ + ____ ⟶

9. **201** = ____ + ____ + ____ ⟶

10. **210** = ____ + ____ + ____ ⟶

11. **299** = ____ + ____ + ____ ⟶

Make your own 200 to 300 chart.

My **200** to **300** Chart

200	210		230			260		280	
201									
202									
					259				
									300

Write the missing numbers.

12. 207, _____ , _____ , _____ , 211, _____ , _____ , 214

13. 259, _____ , 261, _____ , _____ , _____ , 265, _____

What comes before?

14. _____ , 231

15. _____ , 280

16. _____ , 250

between?

17. 269, _____ , 271

18. 298, _____ , 300

19. 223, _____ , 225

after?

20. 250, _____

21. 229, _____

22. 279, _____

★ Test Prep

Which number is between **279** and **281**? Mark the space for your answer.

 23

208   280   278   282
 ○   ○   ○   ○

My **300** to **400** Chart

300	310	320	330	340	350	360	370	380	390
301	311	321	331	341	351	361	371	381	391
302	312	322	332	342	352	362	372	382	392
303	313	323	333	343	353	363	373	383	393
304	314	324	334	344	354	364	374	384	394
305	315	325	335	345	355	365	375	385	395
306	316	326	336	346	356	366	376	386	396
307	317	327	337	347	357	367	377	387	397
308	318	328	338	348	358	368	378	388	398
309	319	329	339	349	359	369	379	389	399
									400

Complete.

1. **383** is _3_ hundreds _8_ tens _3_ ones.

2. **328** is ____ hundreds ____ tens ____ ones.

3. **337** is ____ hundreds ____ tens ____ ones.

4. **379** is ____ hundreds ____ tens ____ ones.

5. **309** is ____ hundreds ____ tens ____ ones.

6. **400** is ____ hundreds ____ tens ____ ones.

7. **346** = _300_ + _40_ + _6_

8. **392** = ____ + ____ + ____

9. **320** = ____ + ____ + ____

10. **311** = ____ + ____ + ____

11. **303** = ____ + ____ + ____

H	T	O
3	4	6
3		
		0
	1	1

Make your own 300 to 400 chart.

My **300** to **400** Chart

300			330					380	
301									
				359					
									400

Write the missing numbers.

12. 309, _____ , 311, _____ , _____ , _____ , _____ , 316

13. _____ , _____ , 371, _____ , _____ , _____ , 375, _____

**Problem Solving
Reasoning**

14. What comes between 311 and 313? Explain how you know._____

_____

★ **Test Prep**

What comes after? Mark the space for your answer.

15

327, ____ | 320   326   328   330
                 ○   ○   ○   ○

My **400** to **500** Chart

400	410	420	430	440	450	460	470	480	490
401	411	421	431	441	451	461	471	481	491
402	412	422	432	442	452	462	472	482	492
403	413	423	433	443	453	463	473	483	493
404	414	424	434	444	454	464	474	484	494
405	415	425	435	445	455	465	475	485	495
406	416	426	436	446	456	466	476	486	496
407	417	427	437	447	457	467	477	487	497
408	418	428	438	448	458	468	478	488	498
409	419	429	439	449	459	469	479	489	499
									500

Write the numbers.

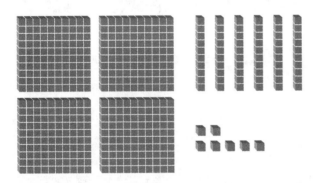

Hundreds	Tens	Ones
4	6	7

$400 + 60 + 7$
$= 467$

Write the numbers.

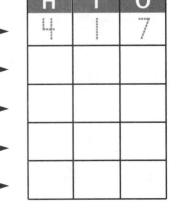

H	T	O
4	1	7

1. $417 = \underline{400} + \underline{10} + \underline{7}$

2. $469 = \underline{} + \underline{} + \underline{}$

3. $433 = \underline{} + \underline{} + \underline{}$

4. $403 = \underline{} + \underline{} + \underline{}$

5. $500 = \underline{} + \underline{} + \underline{}$

Write the missing numbers.

6. 410, ____, ____, ____, 414, ____, ____, ____, 418

7. 453, ____, 455, ____, ____, ____, ____, ____, 461

8. ____, 478, ____, ____, 481, ____, ____, 484, ____

What comes before?	between?	after?
9. ____, 421	11. 477, ____, 479	13. 456, ____
10. ____, 466	12. 490, ____, 492	14. 449, ____

Problem Solving
Reasoning

15. What comes after 468? Explain how you know. _____

_____

_____

☑ **Quick Check**

Write the missing numbers.

1. ____, 238, ____, ____, ____, 242, ____

2. 358, ____, ____, ____, 362, ____, 364

3. ____, 495, ____, 497, ____, ____, ____

Name _____

Complete.

1.

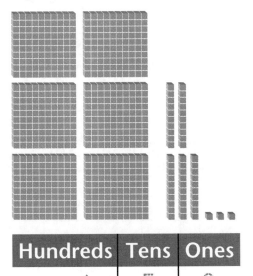

Hundreds	Tens	Ones
6	5	3

$\boxed{6}$ hundreds $\boxed{5}$ tens $\boxed{3}$ ones

or

$\underline{600}$ + $\underline{50}$ + $\underline{3}$

= $\underline{653}$

2.

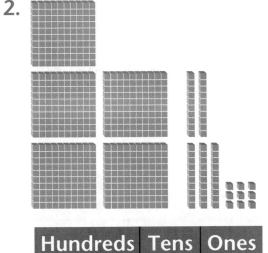

Hundreds	Tens	Ones

$\boxed{}$ hundreds $\boxed{}$ tens $\boxed{}$ ones

or

____ + ____ + ____

= ____

Complete.

3. $200 + 30 + 5 = \boxed{235}$

4. $400 + 50 + 8 = \boxed{}$

5. $500 + 70 + 2 = \boxed{}$

6. $700 + 90 + 7 = \boxed{}$

7. $200 + 0 + 0 = \boxed{}$

8. $300 + 60 + 4 = \boxed{}$

9. $600 + 30 + 0 = \boxed{}$

10. $800 + 0 + 6 = \boxed{}$

Unit 10 • Lesson 7

Complete.

11.

Hundreds	Tens	Ones
9	3	9

☐ hundreds ☐ tens ☐ ones

or

_____ + ____ + ___

= _____

Fill the blanks.

12. **594** is ____ hundreds ____ tens ____ ones.

13. **639** is ____ hundreds ____ tens ____ ones.

14. **945** is ____ hundreds ____ tens ____ ones.

15. **721** is ____ hundreds ____ tens ____ one.

16. **686** is ____ hundreds ____ tens ____ ones.

17. **997** is ____ hundreds ____ tens ____ ones.

18. **753** is ____ hundreds ____ tens ____ ones.

19. **544** is ____ hundreds ____ tens ____ ones.

20. **625** is ____ hundreds ____ tens ____ ones.

21. **809** is ____ hundreds ____ tens ____ ones.

22. **862** is ____ hundreds ____ tens ____ ones.

Complete the chart.

23.

	H	T	O
539	5	3	9
674			
314			
256			
138			
329			
584			
763			
822			

262 (two hundred sixty-two)

Write the missing numbers.

24. 900, 901, _____, _____, _____, _____, _____,

25. 118, _____, _____, _____, _____, _____, _____

26. 732, _____, 734, _____, _____, _____, _____

27. 243, _____, _____, _____, _____, _____, 249

28. 274, _____, _____, _____, _____, _____, _____

29. 303, _____, _____, _____, _____, _____, _____

30. 416, _____, 418, _____, 420, _____, _____

What comes

before?	after?
31. _998_ , 999	32. 786, _787_
_____ , 639	449, _____
_____ , 770	990, _____
_____ , 500	832, _____
_____ , 431	699, _____
_____ , 889	489, _____
_____ , 200	219, _____
_____ , 133	399, _____
_____ , 829	431, _____
_____ , 315	653, _____

Use $>$ or $<$.

33. 177 ◯ 361   301 ◯ 400   211 ◯ 321

34. 454 ◯ 345   413 ◯ 259   155 ◯ 205

35. 201 ◯ 110   164 ◯ 396   499 ◯ 319

36. 322 ◯ 207   246 ◯ 214   388 ◯ 499

Ring the greatest number. | **Ring the least number.**

37. | (386) | 154 | 259 | 236 |

38. | 401 | 743 | 389 | 276 |

39. | 173 | 626 | 418 | (132) |

40. | 198 | 869 | 300 | 279 |

 Problem Solving Reasoning Solve.

41. If you have 9 hundreds, 5 ones, and no tens,

   what is the number?

★ Test Prep

Choose $>$ or $<$.

42

604 ◯ 597

| $>$ | $<$ |
| ◯ | ◯ |

264 (two hundred sixty-four)   Unit 10 • Lesson 7

Name_____

Problem

Look at these numbers
150, 146, 142, 138, 134, 130,___?___
What number is most likely to come next?

1 Understand

I need to find out what number is most likely to come next.

2 Decide

I can look for a pattern using a number chart.

3 Solve

I'll ring the numbers on the chart.

100	110	120	130	140	150	160	170	180	190
101	111	121	131	141	151	161	171	181	191
102	112	122	132	142	152	162	172	182	192
103	113	123	133	143	153	163	173	183	193
104	114	124	134	144	154	164	174	184	194
105	115	125	135	145	155	165	175	185	195
106	116	126	136	146	156	166	176	186	196
107	117	127	137	147	157	167	177	187	197
108	118	128	138	148	158	168	178	188	198
109	119	129	139	149	159	169	179	189	199

I see that each number is 4 less than the last.

I think 126 is most likely to come next.

4 Look back

Does my answer make sense? Why or why not?

Unit 10 • Lesson 8

What number is most likely to come next?
Ring the numbers.
Find a pattern to solve.

1. 322, 327, 332, 337, 342, 347, _____

300	310	320	330	340	350	360	370	380	390
301	311	321	331	341	351	361	371	381	391
302	312	322	332	342	352	362	372	382	392
303	313	323	333	343	353	363	373	383	393
304	314	324	334	344	354	364	374	384	394
305	315	325	335	345	355	365	375	385	395
306	316	326	336	346	356	366	376	386	396
307	317	327	337	347	357	367	377	387	397
308	318	328	338	348	358	368	378	388	398
309	319	329	339	349	359	369	379	389	399

400

2. 229, 227, 225, 223, 221, 219, _____

200	210	220	230	240	250	260	270	280	290
201	211	221	231	241	251	261	271	281	291
202	212	222	232	242	252	262	272	282	292
203	213	223	233	243	253	263	273	283	293
204	214	224	234	244	254	264	274	284	294
205	215	225	235	245	255	265	275	285	295
206	216	226	236	246	256	266	276	286	296
207	217	227	237	247	257	267	277	287	297
208	218	228	238	248	258	268	278	288	298
209	219	229	239	249	259	269	279	289	299

300

Unit 10 • Lesson 8

1¢	5¢	10¢	25¢	50¢

$.01	$.05	$.10	$.25	$.50

Write the amount two ways.

1.

_____ 55 ¢

$ ___.55___

2.

_____ ¢

$ ___.___

3.

_____ ¢

$ ___.___

4.

_____ ¢

$ ___.___

Complete.

5. $.01 = __0__ dimes and __1__ penny.

6. $.02 = __0__ dimes and ____ pennies.

7. $.03 = ____ dimes and ____ pennies.

8. $.04 = ____ dimes and ____ pennies.

9. $.05 = ____ dimes and ____ pennies.

10. $.06 = ____ dimes and ____ pennies.

11. $.07 = ____ dimes and ____ pennies.

12. $.08 = ____ dimes and ____ pennies.

13. $.09 = ____ dimes and ____ pennies.

0 dimes and **4** pennies
4¢ or **$.04**

Write the amount two ways.

14. **0** dimes and **1** penny __$.01__ or __1¢__

15. **0** dimes and **2** pennies _____ or ____

16. **0** dimes and **3** pennies _____ or ____

17. **0** dimes and **4** pennies _____ or ____

18. **0** dimes and **5** pennies _____ or ____

★ Test Prep

Choose >, <, or = . Mark the space for your answer.

19 $.78 ◯ 78¢

>	<	=
◯	◯	◯

10 dimes = $1.00

Complete.

1. two dollars = $ _2.00_   6. **6** dollars and **3** dimes = $ _6.30_

2. eight dollars = $ ___.___   7. **9** dollars and **6** dimes = $ ___.___

3. six dollars = $ ___.___   8. **8** dollars and **4** dimes = $ ___.___

4. five dollars = $ ___.___   9. **$5.50** = _5_ dollars and _5_ dimes

5. three dollars = $ ___.___   10. **$2.40** = ___ dollars and ___ dimes

✓ Quick Check

Write the missing numbers.

1.

299		301	302	

Write the number.

2.

Hundreds	Tens	Ones
6	0	8

= _____

3.

Hundreds	Tens	Ones
4	2	0

= _____

Write the amount two ways.

4. **0** dimes and **7** pennies = _____ or _____¢

Write the amount.

5. **4** dollars and **5** dimes = $ ___.___

Name_____

Complete. Use $.

1.

Dollars	Dimes	Pennies	
2	0	9	= [ ]

2.

Dollars	Dimes	Pennies	
			= [ ]

Fill the blanks.

3. **$9.06** is __9__ dollars __0__ dimes __6__ pennies.

4. **$7.15** is ____ dollars ____ dime ____ pennies.

Write the amount.

5. **2** dollars **0** dimes **7** pennies is $ __2.07__ .

6. **4** dollars **2** dimes **8** pennies is $ ___.___ .

Problem Solving Reasoning | **Ring which is incorrect. Tell why.**

7. **2.75¢**   **$1.25**   **$3.95**

★ Test Prep

How much money? Mark the space for your answer.

8

$1.03 $1.30 $1.21 $1.12
  ○   ○   ○   ○

270 (two hundred seventy)

Unit 10 • Lesson 11

1 half-dollar
$.50
2 half-dollars equal in value **$1.00**

Complete.

1. **1** half-dollar = $ ___.50___

2. **2** half-dollars = $ ___1.00___

3. **3** half-dollars = $ ___.___

4. **4** half-dollars = $ ___.___

5. **5** half-dollars = $ ___.___

6. **6** half-dollars = $ ___.___

Ring the groups that are worth $1.00.

7.

2 quarters equal in value a half-dollar

  =

4 quarters equal in value **$1.00**

  =

Use >, <, or = .

8. 25¢ ⟨ < ⟩ $1.00

9. 75¢ ◯ $.50

10. $1.00 ◯ 4 quarters

11. $1.50 ◯ $2.00

12. $.25 ◯ 25¢

Ring the greatest amount.

13. $.75 ⟨ $1.25 ⟩ $.50

14. $1.00 $2.00 $1.95

15. $4.25 $4.00 $4.50

16. 50¢   75¢ $.55

17. $.25 $.50 $.75

★ **Test Prep**

How much money? Mark the space for your answer.

18

| 78¢ | 86¢ | 71¢ | 96¢ |
| ◯ | ◯ | ◯ | ◯ |

272 (two hundred seventy-two)

Unit 10 • Lesson 12

Use the picture. Solve.

1. Which costs more, paper towels or beans?

Think How much do paper towels cost? $2.00
How much do beans cost? $1.48

$2.00 (>) $1.48

Answer _____

2. Which costs more, oranges or light bulbs?

Think How much do oranges cost?_____
How much do light bulbs cost?_____

_____ ( ) _____

Answer _____

3. Which costs more, beans or sponges?

Think How much do beans cost?_____
How much do sponges cost?_____

_____ ( ) _____

Answer _____

4. Which costs less, peas or paper towels?

Think How much do peas cost?_____
How much do paper towels cost?_____

_____ ( ) _____

Answer _____

Use the picture. Solve.

5. Which costs less, the doll or the top?

_____ ⃝ _____

Answer _____

6. Which costs more, the bowl or the book?

_____ ⃝ _____

Answer _____

7. Which costs more, the ring or the book?

_____ ⃝ _____

Answer _____

8. Which costs less, the plant or the ring?

_____ ⃝ _____

Answer _____

Extend Your Thinking

9. How do you know you found the right answer in problem 8? Explain.

_____

_____

_____

_____

What comes

before? | **between?** | **after?**

1. _____ , 550

2. _____ , 101

3. 299, _____ , 301

4. 909, _____ , 911

5. 109, _____

6. 980, _____

Ring the greatest number.

7. | 927 | 729 | 297 |

8. | 604 | 640 | 146 |

Ring the least number.

9. | 919 | 119 | 991 |

10. | 805 | 508 | 590 |

Complete.

11. **604** is _____ hundreds _____ tens _____ ones.

12. **352** is _____ hundreds _____ tens _____ ones.

Complete.

13. $500 + 30 + 0 =$ ☐

14. $900 + 0 + 8 =$ ☐

15. $400 + 0 + 0 =$ ☐

16. $700 + 60 + 5 =$ ☐

Write the amount two ways.

17.

_____ ¢

$ ____ . ____

18.

_____ ¢

$ ____ . ____

Problem Solving / Reasoning

Use the picture. Solve.

basket
$ .75

candle
2 half-dollars

19. Which costs more, the basket or the candle?

_____ ◯ _____

Answer _____

1

3:40 ○   8:30 ○   8:15 ○   9:15 ○

2

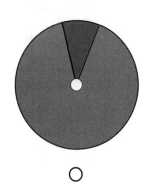   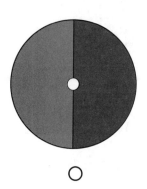   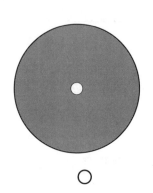

○   ○   ○   ○

3

50075 ○   500705 ○   575 ○   5075 ○

4

847 ○   487 ○   408 ○   87 ○

5

$30.05 ○ $3.50 ○ $3.15 ○ $3.05 ○

Decide on an answer. Mark the space for your answer.
If the answer is **not here**, mark the space for **NH**.

6
```
  27
  20
+ 36
```
☐

○ 73
○ 84
○ 83
○ 74
○ NH

7
```
  57
+ 19
```
☐

○ 69
○ 76
○ 66
○ 75
○ NH

UNIT 11 • TABLE OF CONTENTS

3-Digit Addition and Subtraction

Dear Family,

During the next few weeks our math class will be learning about 3-digit addition and subtraction.

You can expect to see homework that provides practice with adding and subtracting 3-digit numbers.

As we learn about 3-digit addition and subtraction, you may wish to keep the following sample as a guide.

3-Digit Addition with Regrouping

H	T	O
4	5¹	2
+ 1	3	9
5	9	1

Remember to regroup.

11 ones = 1 ten 1 one

H	T	O
5	8¹	5
+ 3	0	8
8	9	3

Regroup.

13 ones = 1 ten 3 ones

3-Digit Subtraction with Regrouping

H	T	O
5	8⁷	²12
− 2	5	9
3	2	3

Remember to regroup a ten.

8 tens 2 ones = 7 tens 12 ones

H	T	O
5	9⁸	¹11
− 4	5	2
1	3	9

Regroup a ten.

9 tens 1 one = 8 tens 11 ones

Sincerely,

Addition   ## Subtraction

H	T	O
3	2	4
+		3
3	2	7

```
  324
+   3
  327
```

H	T	O
9	5	8
–		6
9	5	2

```
  958
–   6
  952
```

Add or subtract.

1.
```
  484        564        846        448        678
–   0      +   3      +   2      –   7      –   5
  484
```

2.
```
  525        931        877        762        432
+   4      –   1      –   2      +   4      –   2
```

★ Test Prep

Solve. Mark the space for your answer.

3
```
  748
–   6
 ┌───┐
 └───┘
```

741   742   745   756
○   ○   ○   ○

Addition

H	T	O
5	6	2
+		1	2
5	7	4

$$\begin{array}{r} 562 \\ +12 \\ \hline 574 \end{array}$$

Subtraction

H	T	O
9	7	6
−		3	5
9	4	1

$$\begin{array}{r} 976 \\ -35 \\ \hline 941 \end{array}$$

Remember to always start with the ones.

Add or subtract.

1.
$$\begin{array}{r} 813 \\ -11 \\ \hline 802 \end{array}$$
$$\begin{array}{r} 403 \\ +92 \\ \hline \end{array}$$
$$\begin{array}{r} 837 \\ -25 \\ \hline \end{array}$$
$$\begin{array}{r} 429 \\ -19 \\ \hline \end{array}$$
$$\begin{array}{r} 667 \\ -42 \\ \hline \end{array}$$

2.
$$\begin{array}{r} 737 \\ -26 \\ \hline \end{array}$$
$$\begin{array}{r} 924 \\ +63 \\ \hline \end{array}$$
$$\begin{array}{r} 890 \\ -50 \\ \hline \end{array}$$
$$\begin{array}{r} 396 \\ -63 \\ \hline \end{array}$$
$$\begin{array}{r} 773 \\ -21 \\ \hline \end{array}$$

3.
$$\begin{array}{r} 439 \\ -25 \\ \hline \end{array}$$
$$\begin{array}{r} 899 \\ -36 \\ \hline \end{array}$$
$$\begin{array}{r} 930 \\ +25 \\ \hline \end{array}$$
$$\begin{array}{r} 430 \\ +50 \\ \hline \end{array}$$
$$\begin{array}{r} 824 \\ -13 \\ \hline \end{array}$$

4.
$$\begin{array}{r} 754 \\ -14 \\ \hline \end{array}$$
$$\begin{array}{r} 296 \\ -73 \\ \hline \end{array}$$
$$\begin{array}{r} 762 \\ -31 \\ \hline \end{array}$$
$$\begin{array}{r} 247 \\ +32 \\ \hline \end{array}$$
$$\begin{array}{r} 524 \\ -13 \\ \hline \end{array}$$

★ Test Prep

Solve. Mark the space for your answer.

5
$$\begin{array}{r} 876 \\ +11 \\ \hline \end{array}$$

865 ○   877 ○   887 ○   986 ○

Add or subtract.

1.

H	T	O
2	1	3
+ 1	6	2
3	7	5

H	T	O
2	4	0
+ 1	1	6

H	T	O
4	5	0
+ 3	4	1

H	T	O
4	5	2
+ 1	2	6

2.

H	T	O
6	6	5
− 3	2	4

H	T	O
8	6	2
− 4	3	0

H	T	O
8	0	5
+ 1	0	3

H	T	O
5	9	8
− 3	7	5

3.

H	T	O
3	9	3
− 1	7	0

H	T	O
9	1	6
− 5	0	1

H	T	O
4	4	1
+ 4	1	7

H	T	O
4	5	6
− 3	5	2

Now try these.

4.

$$785 + 104 = 889$$ $$862 - 430$$ $$450 + 341$$ $$665 - 324$$ $$393 - 173$$

5.

$$258 - 140$$ $$597 + 102$$ $$345 + 142$$ $$986 - 120$$ $$458 - 232$$

Add. Use mental math.

6.
256	683	212	441	500
+ 100	+ 300	+ 300	+ 200	+ 196

7. How does knowing your basic facts help you add in row 6?

_____

Subtract. Use mental math.

8.
616	848	473	352	456
− 500	− 600	− 200	− 300	− 100

9. How does knowing your basic facts help you subtract in row 8?

_____

 Quick Check

Add or subtract.

1.
```
  652
+   7
```

2.
```
  546
−  26
```

3.
```
  314
+ 543
```

4.
```
  879
− 364
```

Name _____

H	T	O
4	5̇	2
+ 1	3	9
5	9	1

Remember
to regroup.

11 ones = **1** ten **1** one

H	T	O
5	8̇	5
+ 3	0	8
8	9	3

Regroup.

13 ones = **1** ten **3** ones

Add.

1.

H	T	O
8	3̇	7
+ 1	2	7
9	6	4

837
+ 127
964

2.

H	T	O
5	4	5
+ 2	2	8

545
+ 228

3.

H	T	O
6	6	6
+ 3	2	6

666
+ 326

4.

H	T	O
8	2	3
+ 1	2	9

823
+ 129

5.

774	137	635	342	426
+ 218	+ 238	+ 136	+ 219	+ 368

6.

369	323	842	256	648
+ 429	+ 259	+ 109	+ 306	+ 237

7.

433	567	336	811	239
+ 239	+ 128	+ 247	+ 109	+ 119

Add.

8.

H	T	O
4	6	7
+ 1	2	4
5	9	1

H	T	O
3	3	3
+ 6	5	9

H	T	O
6	5	4
+ 3	2	9

H	T	O
8	8	7
+ 1	0	7

Find the sum.

9.
$$\begin{array}{r} 448 \\ + 249 \end{array}$$
$$\begin{array}{r} 449 \\ + 339 \end{array}$$
$$\begin{array}{r} 729 \\ + 169 \end{array}$$
$$\begin{array}{r} 638 \\ + 258 \end{array}$$
$$\begin{array}{r} 277 \\ + 619 \end{array}$$

10.
$$\begin{array}{r} 139 \\ + 455 \end{array}$$
$$\begin{array}{r} 646 \\ + 338 \end{array}$$
$$\begin{array}{r} 538 \\ + 345 \end{array}$$
$$\begin{array}{r} 456 \\ + 117 \end{array}$$
$$\begin{array}{r} 766 \\ + 106 \end{array}$$

11.
$$\begin{array}{r} 665 \\ + 119 \end{array}$$
$$\begin{array}{r} 346 \\ + 515 \end{array}$$
$$\begin{array}{r} 234 \\ + 228 \end{array}$$
$$\begin{array}{r} 428 \\ + 415 \end{array}$$
$$\begin{array}{r} 518 \\ + 364 \end{array}$$

Problem Solving
Reasoning

12. If you know that **379 + 363 = 742**, what is the sum of **363 + 379?** Explain. _____

_____

★ **Test Prep**

Solve. Mark the space for your answer.

13.
$$\begin{array}{r} 456 \\ + 228 \\ \hline \square \end{array}$$

228 ○   674 ○   684 ○   685 ○

284 (two hundred eighty-four)

Unit 11 • Lesson 4

Name _____

H	T	O
5	8⁷	2¹²
− 2	5	9
3	2	3

Remember to regroup a ten.

8 tens **2** ones = **7** tens **12** ones

H	T	O
5	9⁸	1¹¹
− 4	5	2
1	3	9

Regroup a ten.

9 tens **1** one = **8** tens **11** ones

Subtract. Remember to regroup the tens and ones.

1.

H	T	O
9	9⁸	2¹²
− 2	1	8
7	7	4

```
  992
− 218
  774
```

2.

H	T	O
4	6⁵	2¹²
− 2	3	4
		8

```
  462
− 234
```

3.

H	T	O
8	4	3
− 4	1	5

```
  843
− 415
```

4.

H	T	O
8	8	2
− 5	1	8

```
  882
− 518
```

5.

```
  573      691      261      535      887
− 117    − 354    − 107    − 126    − 169
```

6.

```
  226      158      666      455      888
− 109    − 109    − 227    − 137    − 269
```

7.

```
  748      261      871      684      816
− 229    − 107    − 639    − 456    − 507
```

Subtract.

8.

H	T	O
5	9̸⁸	1̸¹¹
− 4	6	7

H	T	O
9	9̸⁸	2̸¹²
− 6	5	9

H	T	O
9	8	3
− 6	5	4

H	T	O
8	9	4
− 1	0	7

Find the difference.

9.
$$697 - 448$$ $$788 - 339$$ $$898 - 169$$ $$896 - 638$$ $$896 - 277$$

10.
$$594 - 455$$ $$984 - 646$$ $$893 - 538$$ $$573 - 117$$ $$872 - 766$$

11.
$$784 - 665$$ $$861 - 515$$ $$462 - 234$$ $$843 - 415$$ $$882 - 518$$

Problem Solving Reasoning Solve.

12. There are **362** children and **245** adults at the theater. How many more children than adults are there?

_____ more children

★ Test Prep

Solve. Mark the space for your answer.

13
$$635 - 108 = \boxed{}$$

527 ○   528 ○   537 ○   538 ○

Name_____

$2.43
+ 1.15
$3.58

Add. Don't forget the $ and decimal point.

1.	$5.00 + 2.00 $7.00	$2.00 + 5.00	$3.00 + 5.00	$1.00 + 4.00	$2.00 + 6.00
2.	$1.01 + 2.05 $3.06	$6.03 + 2.04	$3.02 + 3.03	$4.05 + 2.03	$2.04 + 1.05

Subtract. Don't forget the $ and decimal point.

3.	$9.00 − 5.00 $4.00	$7.00 − 3.00	$5.00 − 4.00	$6.00 − 2.00	$4.00 − 1.00
4.	$9.28 − 8.16 $1.12	$6.40 − 4.20	$4.88 − 3.62	$6.35 − 4.11	$7.18 − 7.08

Show your work. Write the answer in a complete sentence.

5. Joe has **$6.00** in his bank. He takes **$3.00** out so that he can buy a present for his mother. How much does he have left in his bank?

$6.00
− 3.00

$

_____

6. Akiko earns **9** dollars, **3** dimes, and **1** nickel, helping her sister on a paper route. She spends **3** dollars and **3** dimes of this money for a new bookmark and saves the rest. How much money does she save?

_____

7. Ted's grandfather gives him **6** dollars, **4** dimes, and **2** nickels. He has **2** dollars, **2** dimes, and **3** nickels in his bank. How much does he have in all?

_____

✓ Quick Check

Add or subtract.

1. 639
   + 232

2. 354
   − 135

3. $8.04
   + 1.77

4. $5.63
   − 2.42

Name_____

Problem

Jeff buys a large sandwich for **$4.15**.
He buys a shake for **$2.25**.
How much money does he spend?

1 Understand

I need to find out how much money Jeff spends.

2 Decide

I can use simpler numbers to help.

3 Solve

If I use simpler numbers the problem would read:
Jeff buys a large sandwich for **$4**.
He buys a shake for **$2**.
How much money does he spend?
I will add to find about how much Jeff spends.
$4 + $2 = $6
I think Jeff spends about **$6**.
Now I will add the amounts.

$$\begin{array}{r} \$4.15 \\ + 2.25 \\ \hline \$6.40 \end{array}$$

Jeff spends **$6.40**.

4 Look back

I know that my answer should be about **$6** and it is **$6.40**.

First solve the problem with simpler numbers.
Use it to solve the next problem.

1. Ké has **$4**. He buys a large sandwich for **$2**. How much money does he have left?

Ké has **$4.15**. He buys a large sandwich for **$2.12**. How much money does he have left?

2. Mary Lou buys a fish sandwich for **$2** and a small order of french fries for **$1**. How much does she spend?

Mary Lou buys a fish sandwich for **$2.05** and a small order of french fries for **$.85**. How much does she spend?

3. Mark spends **$6**. Jenna spends **$5**. How much more does Mark spend than Jenna?

Mark spends **$6.25**. Jenna spends **$5.35**. How much more does Mark spend than Jenna?

Name _____

| Problem Solving Plan |
| 1. Understand 2. Decide 3. Solve 4. Look back |

Solve.

1. Jan has **$1.79**. She buys a marker for **$.68**. How much does she have left?

Answers

Think Jan starts with ____$1.79____ .

How much does the marker cost? ____$ .68____

Do you add or subtract? ____subtract____

$1.79
− .68
----

2. Raul buys a toy car for **$4.29** and a truck for **$5.15**. How much money does he spend?

Think How much does the toy car cost? _____

How much does the truck cost? _____

Do you add or subtract? _____

3. Leah has **8** dollar bills, **2** quarters, **2** dimes, **1** nickel, and **5** pennies. She buys a model airplane for **$5.36**. How much money does she have left?

Think: Leah starts with _____ .

How much does the airplane cost? _____

Do you add or subtract? _____

Think about whether you need to add or subtract. Solve.

Answers

4. Eric has **$6.15**. He wants to buy a book that costs **$7.20**. How much more money does he need?

5. Mei-Mei wants to buy a doll that costs **$9.48**. She gives the clerk **9** dollar bills, **1** quarter, **2** dimes, and **1** nickel. How much money does the clerk give back to Mei-Mei?

6. Anthony wants to buy a toy airplane that costs **$4.79** and a bottle of glue that costs **$1.19**. How much money does he need?

Extend Your Thinking

7. Rachel has **$2.00** to spend. A pen costs **79¢**, a notepad **89¢**, and an eraser **49¢**.
   What is the greatest number of pens Rachel can buy? Notepads? Erasers?

   Workspace

   _____ pens   _____ notepads   _____ erasers

   Explain how you know the number of erasers you can buy.

Add or subtract. Watch the signs.
Remember to always start with the ones.

1. 261
  − 107

2. 871
  − 256

3. 784
  + 113

4. 893
  − 166

5. 573
  + 119

6. 748
  − 219

7. 229
  + 348

8. 267
  + 126

9. 685
  − 263

10. 147
  + 237

11. 519
  + 228

12. 446
  + 223

13. 234
  + 349

14. 729
  + 169

15. 728
  + 139

Add or subtract.

16. $1.48
  + 2.48

17. $8.37
  + 1.58

18. $4.49
  + 2.41

19. $6.88
  − 1.79

20. $5.47
  − 2.38

Problem Solving Reasoning Solve.

Answers

21. Martha buys a hat for **$6.27** and a pin for **$2.13**. How much money does she spend?

22. Hans has **9** dollar bills, **2** quarters, **1** dime, **3** nickels, and **6** pennies. He buys a baseball cap for **$8.50**. How much money does he have left?

Name _____

1

I day = _____ hours   24   30   60   90
                          ○   ○   ○   ○

2

68   683   63   638
○   ○   ○   ○

3

756   76   765   75
○   ○   ○   ○

4

$ .56 $6.50 $ .65 $6.05
○   ○   ○   ○

5

$6.50	$6.50	$3.25	$3.25
− 3.25	− 3.00	+ 3.25	+ 3.50
$3.25	$3.50	$6.50	$6.75
○	○	○	○

Decide on an answer. Mark the space for your answer.
If the answer is **not here**, mark the space **NH.**

6

74
− 26
☐   47   48   57   58   NH
           ○   ○   ○   ○   ○

UNIT 12 • TABLE OF CONTENTS

Multiplication and Division

Dear Family,

During the next few weeks our math class will be learning about multiplication and division.

You can expect to see homework that provides practice with multiplication and division.

As we learn about multiplication, you may wish to keep the following sample as a guide.

3 groups of **2**

Write: $3 \times 2 = 6$ or

$$\begin{array}{r} 2 \quad \text{factor} \\ \times\ 3 \quad \text{factor} \\ \hline 6 \quad \text{product} \end{array}$$

factor factor product

Sincerely,

Skip-count. Fill in the blanks.

1.

___2___ , ___4___

__2__ groups of **2**

__4__ in all

2.

____ group of **2**

____ in all

_____

3.

____ groups of **2**

____ in all

____ , ____ , ____ , ____

4.

____ groups of **2**

____ in all

____ , ____ , ____

★ Test Prep

How many groups of **2**? Mark your answer.

| 1 | 2 | 3 | 4 |
| ○ | ○ | ○ | ○ |

Fill in the blanks.

1.      _4_ groups of _2_

   _8_ in all

   _2_ + _2_ + _2_ + _2_

2.   ___ groups of ___

   ___ in all

   ___ + ___ + ___ + ___ + ___ + ___ + ___

3.     ___ groups of ___

   ___ in all

   ___ + ___ + ___ + ___ + ___

4.   ___ groups of _2_

   ___ in all

5. 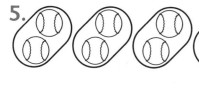 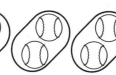 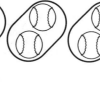   ___ groups of ___

   ___ in all

   ___ + ___ + ___ + ___ + ___ + ___ + ___ + ___

★ **Test Prep**

How many in all? Mark the space for your answer.

6.

| 8 | 10 | 12 | 14 |
| ○ | ○ | ○ | ○ |

Name _____

The picture shows **3** groups of **2**. There are **6** dots in all.

You say: **3** times **2** equals **6**.

You write: **3 × 2 = 6**

↖ This sign tells you to multiply.

Draw groups of dots. Complete the number sentence.

1.

   $1 × 2 = \underline{\quad 2 \quad}$

2.

   $2 × 2 = \underline{\quad\quad}$

3.

   $3 × 2 = \underline{\quad\quad}$

4.

   $4 × 2 = \underline{\quad\quad}$

5.

   $5 × 2 = \underline{\quad\quad}$

6.

   $6 × 2 = \underline{\quad\quad}$

7.

   $7 × 2 = \underline{\quad\quad}$

8.

   $8 × 2 = \underline{\quad\quad}$

9.

   $9 × 2 = \underline{\quad\quad}$

The **array** has **3** rows of **2**.

Write: **3 × 2 = 6**   or

$$\begin{array}{r} 2 \\ \times\,3 \\ \hline 6 \end{array}$$ factor
factor
product

factor   factor   product

Find the product.

10. $\times 4$ **2** 8

11. $\times 5$ **2**

12. $\times 6$ **2**

13. $\times 7$ **2**

Skip-count. Fill in the blanks.

1.
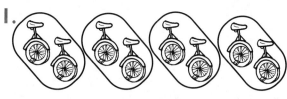

___ groups of **2**

____ , ____ , ____ , ____   ___ in all

2.
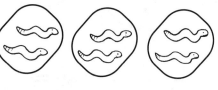

___ groups of **2**

____ + ____ + ____   ___ in all

Find the product.

3.
   $\times 2$ **2**

300 (three hundred)

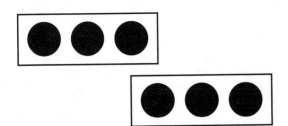

There are **2** groups.
There are **3** objects in each group.
There are **6** objects in all.

Write: **2 × 3 = 6**   or   **× 2**
$$\begin{array}{r} 3 \\ \times\ 2 \\ \hline 6 \end{array}$$

Multiply.

1.

$$\begin{array}{r} 3 \\ \times\ 3 \\ \hline \end{array}$$

3 × 3 = __9__

2.

$$\begin{array}{r} 3 \\ \times\ 4 \\ \hline \end{array}$$

4 × 3 = ____

3.

$$\begin{array}{r} 3 \\ \times\ 5 \\ \hline \end{array}$$

5 × 3 = ____

4.

$$\begin{array}{r} 3 \\ \times\ 1 \\ \hline \end{array}$$

1 × 3 = ____

5.

$$\begin{array}{r} 3 \\ \times\ 0 \\ \hline \end{array}$$

0 × 3 = ____

Find the product.

6.
$\begin{array}{r} 1 \\ \times 2 \\ \hline 2 \end{array}$
$\begin{array}{r} 8 \\ \times 2 \\ \hline \end{array}$
$\begin{array}{r} 2 \\ \times 2 \\ \hline \end{array}$
$\begin{array}{r} 3 \\ \times 1 \\ \hline \end{array}$
$\begin{array}{r} 3 \\ \times 0 \\ \hline \end{array}$
$\begin{array}{r} 2 \\ \times 7 \\ \hline \end{array}$

7.
$\begin{array}{r} 7 \\ \times 2 \\ \hline \end{array}$
$\begin{array}{r} 3 \\ \times 3 \\ \hline \end{array}$
$\begin{array}{r} 1 \\ \times 3 \\ \hline \end{array}$
$\begin{array}{r} 2 \\ \times 6 \\ \hline \end{array}$
$\begin{array}{r} 2 \\ \times 8 \\ \hline \end{array}$
$\begin{array}{r} 6 \\ \times 2 \\ \hline \end{array}$

8.
$\begin{array}{r} 4 \\ \times 3 \\ \hline \end{array}$
$\begin{array}{r} 2 \\ \times 5 \\ \hline \end{array}$
$\begin{array}{r} 4 \\ \times 2 \\ \hline \end{array}$
$\begin{array}{r} 2 \\ \times 9 \\ \hline \end{array}$
$\begin{array}{r} 0 \\ \times 2 \\ \hline \end{array}$
$\begin{array}{r} 2 \\ \times 8 \\ \hline \end{array}$

9.
$\begin{array}{r} 0 \\ \times 3 \\ \hline \end{array}$
$\begin{array}{r} 3 \\ \times 2 \\ \hline \end{array}$
$\begin{array}{r} 3 \\ \times 4 \\ \hline \end{array}$
$\begin{array}{r} 5 \\ \times 3 \\ \hline \end{array}$
$\begin{array}{r} 3 \\ \times 6 \\ \hline \end{array}$
$\begin{array}{r} 2 \\ \times 3 \\ \hline \end{array}$

10.
$\begin{array}{r} 3 \\ \times 5 \\ \hline \end{array}$
$\begin{array}{r} 1 \\ \times 3 \\ \hline \end{array}$
$\begin{array}{r} 2 \\ \times 1 \\ \hline \end{array}$
$\begin{array}{r} 2 \\ \times 4 \\ \hline \end{array}$
$\begin{array}{r} 5 \\ \times 2 \\ \hline \end{array}$
$\begin{array}{r} 9 \\ \times 2 \\ \hline \end{array}$

Problem Solving
Reasoning

11. If you multiply any number by **1**, what is the product?
How do you know? _____

_____

★ **Test Prep**

Multiply. Mark the space for your answer.

12
$\begin{array}{r} 6 \\ \times 3 \\ \hline \end{array}$

| 9 | 12 | 15 | 18 |
| ○ | ○ | ○ | ○ |

Name _____

Complete.

1.   __1__ group of __5__

                                                   __5__ in all

2.   ____ groups of ____

                                                   _____ in all

3.   ____ groups of ____

                                                   _____ in all

4.   ____ groups of ____

                                                   _____ in all

5.   ____ groups of ____

                                                   _____ in all

Find the product.

6. $1 \times 5 =$ __5__   7. $0 \times 5 =$ _____   8. $2 \times 5 =$ _____

9. $5 \times 3 =$ _____   10. $5 \times 5 =$ _____   11. $5 \times 4 =$ _____

Unit 12 • Lesson 5

Draw an array of 2 rows of 5.

12.

*	*	*	*	*
*	*	*	*	*

$2 \times 5 =$ _____

Draw an array of 5 rows of 2.

13.

$5 \times 2 =$ _____

Practice your facts. Solve.

14.

$\begin{array}{r} 5 \\ \times 6 \\ \hline \end{array}$
$\begin{array}{r} 2 \\ \times 5 \\ \hline \end{array}$
$\begin{array}{r} 3 \\ \times 0 \\ \hline \end{array}$
$\begin{array}{r} 5 \\ \times 8 \\ \hline \end{array}$
$\begin{array}{r} 5 \\ \times 7 \\ \hline \end{array}$
$\begin{array}{r} 2 \\ \times 6 \\ \hline \end{array}$
$\begin{array}{r} 3 \\ \times 7 \\ \hline \end{array}$
$\begin{array}{r} 5 \\ \times 9 \\ \hline \end{array}$

Problem Solving Reasoning

15. If you multiply any number by **0**, what is the product?
How do you know? _____

_____

★ Test Prep

Multiply. Mark the space for your answer.

16

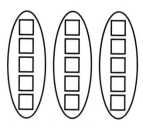

18	15	12	8
○	○	○	○

$3 \times 5 = \boxed{}$

304 (three hundred four)

Name _____

Problem

Keith makes **2** piles of books on the shelf.
He puts **4** books in each pile.
How many books are there?

---

1 **Understand**

I need to find out how many books there are in all.

2 **Decide**

I can act it out.

3 **Solve**

I'll use counters instead of books.
I'll make **2** piles of **4** books.

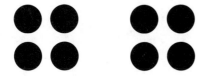

There are ___8___ books.

4 **Look back**

I know **2** groups of **4** equal **8** or **2 x 4 = 8**.
My answer makes sense.

Use counters. Act it out to solve.

1. Toby sees **2** groups of girls playing. There are **3** girls in each group. How many girls does she see in all?

_____ girls

2. There are **4** girls. Each girl has **3** marbles. How many marbles do they have in all?

_____ marbles

3. Julie put **3** rows of papers on the desk. If she puts **3** papers in each row, how many papers does she put on the desk?

_____ papers

4. Pedro puts **3** rows of pencils on the table with **5** in each row. How many pencils does Pedro put on the table?

_____ pencils

5. In which problems did you put counters in arrays? Why? _____

_____

_____

**Ring the operation.
Write the number sentence. Solve.**

1. 1 bicycle has **2** wheels. How many wheels are there on **5** bicycles?

   Think

   add   subtract   (multiply)

   $2 \times 5 = 10$
   _____

   __10__ wheels

2. If **1** stool has **3** legs, how many legs are there on **6** stools?

   Think

   add   subtract   multiply

   _____

   _____ legs

3. Ari has **3** books. Pam has **2** books. How many books do they have all together?

   Think

   add   subtract   multiply

   _____

   _____ books

4. Ray needs **7** cans of juice. He already has **3** cans. How many more cans does he need?

   Think

   add   subtract   multiply

   _____

   _____ cans

Ring the operation.
Write a number sentence. Solve.

5. **1** week has **7** days. How
   many days are there in **3**
   weeks?

   _____

   add   subtract   multiply   _____ days

---

6. There are **30** days in April.
   There are **31** days in May.
   How many days are there in
   April and May?

   _____

   _____ days

   add   subtract   multiply

---

7. If **1** flower has **5** petals, how
   many petals are there on **9**
   flowers?

   _____

   _____ petals

   add   subtract   multiply

Extend Your Thinking

8. Choose one of the problems on this page. Show how you can check
   your answer to make sure it is correct.

Name _____

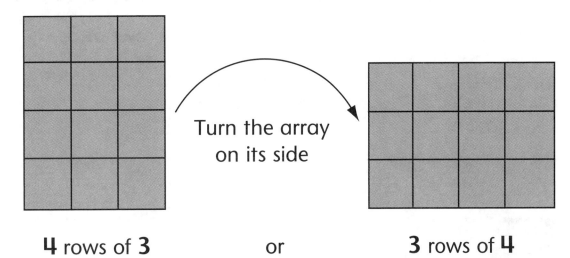

4 rows of **3**   or   **3** rows of **4**
4 × 3 = 12   **3 × 4 = 12**

Use grid paper. Color squares to show the number in each row.
Then turn the paper. Complete the number sentences.

1.
    3 rows of **5**   **5** rows of **3**

   __3__ × __5__ = __15__   or   _____ × _____ = _____

2.
    4 rows of **1**   **1** row of **4**

   _____ × _____ = _____   or   _____ × _____ = _____

3.
    0 rows of **3**   **3** rows of **0**

   _____ × _____ = _____   or   _____ × _____ = _____

4.
    2 rows of **4**   **4** rows of **2**

   _____ × _____ = _____   or   _____ × _____ = _____

Continue using grid paper to complete the number sentences.

5.   **5** rows of **4**   **4** rows of **5**

_____ × _____ = _____   or   _____ × _____ = _____

6.   **1** row of **3**   **3** rows of **1**

_____ × _____ = _____   or   _____ × _____ = _____

Problem Solving Reasoning

7. How is multiplying **3 × 2** the same as multiplying **2 × 3**?

Explain. _____

_____

_____

✓ Quick Check

Multiply.

1. $4 \times 3 =$ ____

2. $6 \times 5 =$ ____

Write the number sentences.

3. 3 rows of **6**   **6** rows of **3**

____ × ____ = ____ or ____ × ____ = ____

310 (three hundred ten)   **Unit 12 • Lesson 8**

Name _____

Fill the blanks.

1.

        __1__ group of __10__

        __10__ in all

2.

        _____ groups of _____

        _____ in all

3.

        _____ groups of _____

        _____ in all

4.

        _____ groups of _____

        _____ in all

5.

        _____ groups of _____

        _____ in all

Find the product.

6.
$$\begin{array}{r} 10 \\ \times\ 5 \\ \hline \end{array} \qquad \begin{array}{r} 10 \\ \times\ 8 \\ \hline \end{array} \qquad \begin{array}{r} 10 \\ \times\ 1 \\ \hline \end{array} \qquad \begin{array}{r} 10 \\ \times\ 6 \\ \hline \end{array} \qquad \begin{array}{r} 10 \\ \times\ 2 \\ \hline \end{array} \qquad \begin{array}{r} 10 \\ \times\ 9 \\ \hline \end{array}$$

★ Test Prep

Find the product. Mark the space for your answer.

7

$4 \times 10 = \boxed{}$

30	14	40	6
○	○	○	○

Name_____

A multiplication table shows the products of one factor and a series of other factors. Here's a multiplication table for 3.

factor ⟶

×	③
0	0
1	3
②	⑥
3	9
4	12
5	15
6	18

⟵ factor

⟵ product

Complete.

1.

×	2
0	0
1	2
2	4
3	6
4	
5	
6	
7	14
8	
9	18
10	

2.

×	5
0	
1	
2	
3	
4	
5	25
6	
7	
8	
9	
10	

3.

×	10
0	
1	
2	
3	
4	
5	
6	
7	
8	
9	
10	100

★ Test Prep

Find the product. Mark the space for your answer.

$2 \times 7 = \boxed{}$

12	16	14	9
○	○	○	○

Name _____

Birds Seen at White Lake

Each 🐦 stands for **5** birds.

**How many birds were seen by each person?
Complete the number sentences.**

1. Frank __2__ × __5__ = __10__   4. José ____ × ____ = _____

2. Mae ____ × ____ = _____   5. Tim ____ × ____ = _____

3. Iris ____ × ____ = _____   6. Rosa ____ × ____ = _____

Solve.

7. How many birds did Mae and Iris see altogether?

   __30__ birds

8. How many birds did José and Tim see altogether?

   _____ birds

Cans of Juice Sold

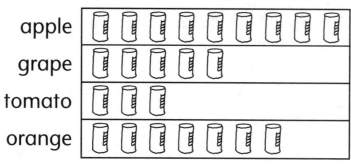

Each 🥫 stands for **10** cans.

How many cans of each type of juice were sold?
Complete the number sentences.

9. apple ___9___ × ___10___ = ___90___ | 11. tomato ____ × ____ = ____

10. grape ____ × ____ = ____ | 12. orange ____ × ____ = ____

Problem Solving
Reasoning

13. Write a number sentence that shows how many cans of grape

juice and tomato juice were sold altogether. _____

✓ Quick Check

Find the product.

1. 6 × 10 = ____

Complete.

2.

×	5
0	
1	
	10
	15
4	

Solve.

3. **Balloons Sold**

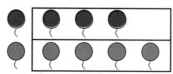

Each ○ stands for **5** balloons.

How many red balloons were sold?

____ × ____ = ____

Name_____

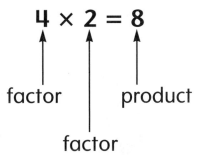

$$4 \times 2 = 8$$

factor   factor   product

Find the missing factor.

1.   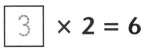 $\boxed{3} \times 2 = 6$

2.    $\boxed{} \times 2 = 8$

3. $\boxed{} \times 2 = 0$

4.    $3 \times \boxed{} = 6$

5.  $1 \times \boxed{} = 2$

6.    $\boxed{} \times 2 = 4$

7.     $4 \times \boxed{} = 8$

8.  $\boxed{} \times 2 = 12$

Find the missing factor.

9.  $\boxed{} \times 2 = 2$

10. $\boxed{} \times 3 = 9$

11.  $\boxed{} \times 5 = 20$

12. $\boxed{} \times 2 = 10$

13. $6 \times \boxed{} = 18$

14. 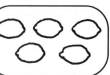 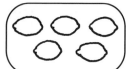 $2 \times \boxed{} = 10$

15. $8 \times \boxed{} = 24$

16. $\boxed{} \times 2 = 18$

★ Test Prep

Solve. Mark the space for your answer.

17 $7 \times \boxed{} = 21$

    2   3   5   4
    ○   ○   ○   ○

Unit 12 • Lesson 12

Name _____

Ring equal groups.
Write the number in each group.

1.

9 is **3** groups of ___*3*___ .

2.

8 is **2** groups of ____ .

3.

15 is **5** groups of ____ .

4.

16 is **4** groups of ____ .

5.

15 is **3** groups of ____ .

6.

10 is **5** groups of ____ .

7.

4 is **2** groups of ____ .

8.

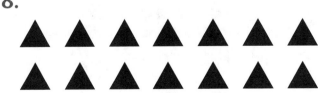

14 is **2** groups of ____ .

Ring equal groups.
Write the number in each group.

9.

8 is **4** groups of ___2___ .

10.

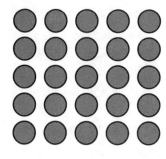

25 is **5** groups of _____ .

11.

12 is **4** groups of _____ .

12.

12 is **2** groups of _____ .

13.

20 is **5** groups of _____ .

14.

12 is **3** groups of _____ .

★ Test Prep

Solve. Mark the space for your answer.

15

10 is **2** groups of ☐ .

10	5	4	2
○	○	○	○

Name _____

Tara has **8** shells.
She wants to give **2** shells to each friend.
How many friends will get shells?

$$
\begin{array}{r} 8 \\ -2 \\ \hline 6 \end{array}
\quad
\begin{array}{r} 6 \\ -2 \\ \hline 4 \end{array}
\quad
\begin{array}{r} 4 \\ -2 \\ \hline 2 \end{array}
\quad
\begin{array}{r} 2 \\ -2 \\ \hline 0 \end{array}
$$

You subtract **4** times.

4 friends will each get **2** shells.

Complete.

1. There are **10** children going sledding.
   Each sled holds **2** children.
   How many sleds do they need?

$$
\begin{array}{r} 10 \\ -2 \\ \hline 8 \end{array}
\quad
\begin{array}{r} 8 \\ -2 \\ \hline 6 \end{array}
\quad
\begin{array}{r} 6 \\ -2 \\ \hline 4 \end{array}
\quad
\begin{array}{r} 4 \\ -2 \\ \hline 2 \end{array}
\quad
\begin{array}{r} 2 \\ -2 \\ \hline 0 \end{array}
$$

You subtract __5__ times.

They need __5__ sleds.

2. Renée has **6** toy bears.
   She wants to put **2** bears on each chair.
   How many chairs will she use?

$$
\begin{array}{r} 6 \\ -2 \\ \hline 4 \end{array}
\quad
\begin{array}{r} 4 \\ -2 \\ \hline 2 \end{array}
\quad
\begin{array}{r} 2 \\ -2 \\ \hline 0 \end{array}
$$

You subtract _____ times.

Renée will use _____ chairs.

Unit 12 • Lesson 14

(three hundred nineteen) 319

Complete.

3. Sam has **8** marbles.
   He wants to give **2** to each friend.
   How many friends will get marbles?

   You subtract __4__ times.

   _____ friends will each get **2** marbles.

Find the missing factor.

1.

   3 × [ ] = 9

Ring equal groups.
Write the number in each group.

2.

   12 is **3** groups of _____ .

Complete the sentences.

3. Anika has **6** books.
   She wants to put **2** books on each shelf.
   How many shelves will she use?

   You subtract _____ times.

   Anika will use _____ shelves.

320 (three hundred twenty)

Unit 12 • Lesson 14

Fill in the blanks.

1. __10__ fish

Ring groups of **3**.

__3__ groups

__1__ left over

2. _____ birds

Ring groups of **5**.

_____ groups

_____ left over

3. _____ frogs

Ring groups of **2**.

_____ groups

_____ left over

4. _____ starfish

Ring groups of **3**.

_____ groups

_____ left over

Fill in the blanks.

5. _____ nests

Ring groups of **2**.

   _____ groups

   _____ left over

6. _____ dragonflies

Ring groups of **5**.

   _____ groups

   _____ left over

| **Problem Solving** |
| **Reasoning** |

Solve.

7. Mi Lee wants to store her marble collection in bags.
A shop sells bags that will hold up to **10** marbles.
Mi Lee has **38** marbles.
What are the fewest number of bags she needs to buy?

_____

_____

★ **Test Prep**

How many are left over? Mark the space for your answer.

8

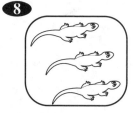 

0	1	2	3
○	○	○	○

Name _____

Skip-count. Fill in the blanks.

1.

____ , ____ , ____

____ groups of ____

____ in all

2.

____ , ____ , ____ , ____

____ groups of ____

____ in all

3.

____ , ____ , ____ , ____ , ____

____ groups of ____

____ in all

Find the product.

4. $\begin{array}{r} 2 \\ \times\, 3 \\ \hline \end{array}$

5. $\begin{array}{r} 7 \\ \times\, 2 \\ \hline \end{array}$

Find the product.

6. $\begin{array}{r} 2 \\ \times\, 3 \\ \hline \end{array}$
7. $\begin{array}{r} 4 \\ \times\, 2 \\ \hline \end{array}$
8. $\begin{array}{r} 10 \\ \times\, 2 \\ \hline \end{array}$
9. $\begin{array}{r} 3 \\ \times\, 7 \\ \hline \end{array}$
10. $\begin{array}{r} 5 \\ \times\, 3 \\ \hline \end{array}$
11. $\begin{array}{r} 6 \\ \times\, 2 \\ \hline \end{array}$

12. $\begin{array}{r} 2 \\ \times\, 8 \\ \hline \end{array}$
13. $\begin{array}{r} 10 \\ \times\, 9 \\ \hline \end{array}$
14. $\begin{array}{r} 5 \\ \times\, 4 \\ \hline \end{array}$
15. $\begin{array}{r} 10 \\ \times\, 0 \\ \hline \end{array}$
16. $\begin{array}{r} 5 \\ \times\, 5 \\ \hline \end{array}$
17. $\begin{array}{r} 10 \\ \times\, 5 \\ \hline \end{array}$

Ring equal groups.
Write the number in each group.

18.

9 is **3** groups of _____ .

19.

25 is **5** groups of _____ .

20.

10 is **5** groups of _____ .

21.

16 is **2** groups of _____ .

22.

12 is **3** groups of _____ .

23.

4 is **2** groups of _____ .

Ring the operation.
Write a number sentence. Solve.

24. One cat has **4** legs.

How many legs are there on

3 cats?   _____

add   subtract   multiply   _____ legs

324 (three hundred twenty-four)   Unit 12 • Review

1

○ **9** o'clock   ○ quarter past **4**

○ quarter to **4**   ○ quarter past **9**

2

I year = _____ months

| 6 | 12 | 24 | 30 |
| ○ | ○ | ○ | ○ |

3

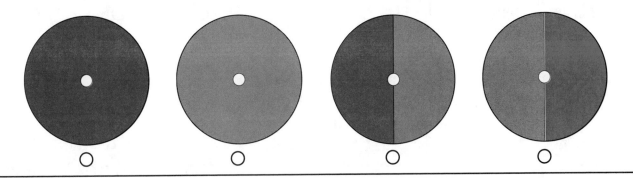

○   ○   ○   ○

4

| 248 | 2048 | 200408 | 20048 |
| ○ | ○ | ○ | ○ |

5

| 639 | 60309 | 60039 | 600309 |
| ○ | ○ | ○ | ○ |

6

| $8.95 | $5.98 | $5.908 | $5.89 |
| ○ | ○ | ○ | ○ |

7

23 ◯ 18 = 5

+	−	>	<
◯	◯	◯	◯

8

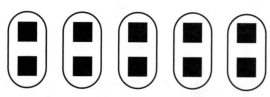

5 groups of **2** or ▢ in all.

2	5	10	20
◯	◯	◯	◯

9

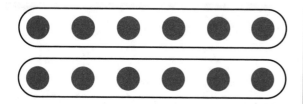

12 is **2** groups of ▢.

12	8	6	5
◯	◯	◯	◯

10

Decide on an answer. Mark the space for your answer.
If the answer is **not here**, mark the space for **NH**.

10 × 0 = ▢

0	1	10	100	NH
◯	◯	◯	◯	◯

11

```
  35
+ 57
┌────┐
│    │
└────┘
```

○ 83
○ 82
○ 93
○ 92
○ NH

12

```
  73
- 54
┌────┐
│    │
└────┘
```

○ 29
○ 28
○ 19
○ 18
○ NH

Unit 12 • Cumulative Review

add

3 + 4 = 7

between

35, 36, 37

36 is between **35** and **37**.

addend

3 + 5 = 8

addends

cent (¢)

 = 1¢

after

39, 40

40 is after **39**.

centimeter a metric unit of length

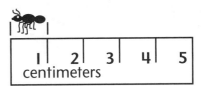

bar graph

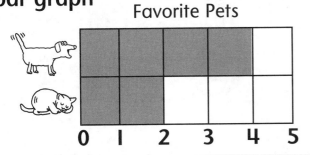

circle

before

33, 34

33 is before **34**.

cone

Picture Glossary

congruent

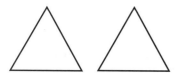

These triangles are congruent.
They are the same size and shape

day

8:00 AM   8:00 PM   8:00 AM

There are 24 hours in a day.

corner

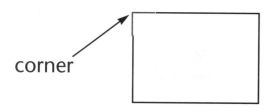

corner

difference

$$8 - 4 = 4 \qquad \begin{array}{r} 8 \\ -\ 4 \\ \hline 4 \end{array}$$

difference

cube

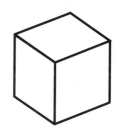

digit

tens digit

46

ones digit

46 has two digits.

cup a customary unit of capacity

dime

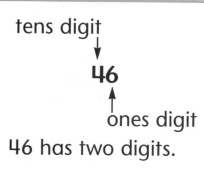

10¢   10 cents

cylinder

dollar

100¢ or $1.00

Picture Glossary

edge

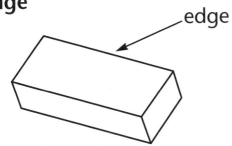

edge

fact family

$$3 + 6 = 9 \quad 6 + 3 = 9$$

$$9 - 3 = 6 \quad 9 - 6 = 3$$

is equal to

$$4 = 4$$

4 is equal to **4**.

foot a customary unit of length

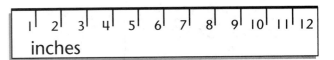

12 inches equal **1** foot.

estimate

about 20 shells

factor

$$3 \times 2 = 6$$

factors

expanded form

$$245 = 200 + 40 + 5$$

fourths

| $\frac{1}{4}$ | $\frac{1}{4}$ |
| $\frac{1}{4}$ | $\frac{1}{4}$ |

4 fourths equal a whole.

face

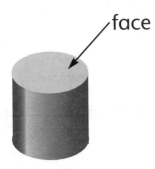

face

fraction

one-half   one-third   one-fourth

Picture Glossary

gallon a customary unit of capacity

4 quarts equal **1** gallon.

halves

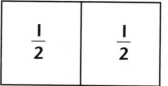

2 halves equal a whole.

is greater than

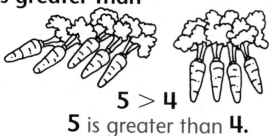

5 > 4

5 is greater than **4.**

hour

There are 60 minutes in an hour.

grouping property

$$3 + (2 + 3) = 8$$

$$(3 + 2) + 3 = 8$$

hundreds

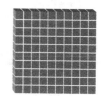

3 hundreds

half dollar

50¢   **50** cents

inch

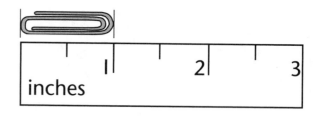

half hour

30 minutes equals **1** half hour.

kilogram a metric unit of mass

The book is about **1** kilogram.

Picture Glossary

is less than

$3 < 5$

3 is less than **5**.

mode the number that occurs most often

1   2   2   3   4   5

2 is the mode.

line of symmetry

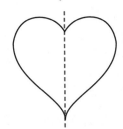

month

There are 12 months in a year.

liter (L)

multiplication sentence

$6 \times 3 = 18$

meter a metric unit of measurement

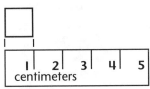

centimeters

100 centimeters equal **1** meter.

multiply

$4 \times 2 = 8$

minute

There are **60** seconds in a minute.

nickel

5¢   5 cents

Picture Glossary

number sentence

$$8 + 2 = 10$$

$$6 - 4 = 2$$

picture graph

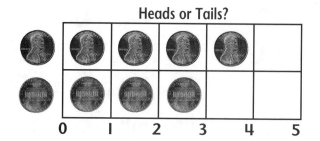

ones

5 ones

pint a customary unit of capacity

2 cups equal **1** pint.

order property

$$3 + 4 = 7$$

$$4 + 3 = 7$$

place value the value of each place

Tens	Ones
3	4

In **34** the digit **3** is in the tens place.

pattern

3, 5, 7, 9, 11, __?__

pound a customary unit of weight

The butter weighs about **1** pound.

penny

1¢   1 cent

product

$$5 \times 3 = 15$$

$$\begin{array}{r} 3 \\ \times\, 5 \\ \hline 15 \end{array}$$

product

Picture Glossary

quart a customary unit of capacity

2 pints equal **1** quart.

rectangle

quarter

25¢   **25** cents

rectangular prism

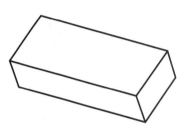

quarter past

quarter past **11** or **11:15**

regroup

10 ones equal **1** ten.

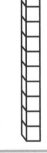

quarter to

quarter to **4** or **3:45**

related facts

$$9 + 1 = 10$$
$$10 - 1 = 9$$

range the difference between the least and the greatest numbers

1 2 3 4 5 6

$$6 - 1 = 5$$
range

second

It takes about **1** second to snap.

Picture Glossary

skip-count

sum

$6 + 3 = 9$

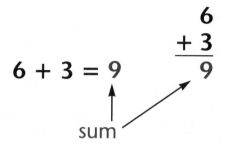

sum

sphere

tens

4 tens

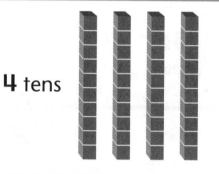

square

thirds

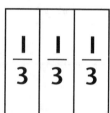

square pyramid

triangle

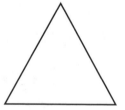

subtract

$5 - 2 = 3$

week

Sunday, Monday, Tuesday, Wednesday, Thursday, Friday, Saturday

There are **7** days in a week.